U18920132 1087

D0434888

Twayne's New Critical Introductions
to Shakespeare

ALL'S WELL THAT
ENDS WELL

Twayne's New Critical Introductions to Shakespeare

ALL'S WELL THAT ENDS WELL

Sheldon P. Zitner

Professor of English
Trinity College
University of Toronto

TWAYNE PUBLISHERS · BOSTON
A Division of G. K. Hall & Co.

Published in the United States by Twayne Publishers
A Division of G. K. Hall & Co.
70 Lincoln Street
Boston, Massachusetts 02111

Published simultaneously in Great Britain by
Harvester Wheatsheaf
66 Wood Lane End, Hemel Hempstead, Herts.

Twayne's New Critical Introductions to Shakespeare, no. 10

Library of Congress Cataloging-in-Publication Data

Zitner, Sheldon P.
    All's well that ends well / Sheldon Zitner.
        p.   cm. — (Twayne's new critical introductions to
Shakespeare)
    Includes bibliographical references.
    ISBN 0-8057-8718-6. — ISBN 0-8057-8719-4 (pbk.)
    1. Shakespeare, William, 1564–1616.   All's well that ends well.
I. Title.   II. Series.
PR2801.Z58   1989
822.3'3—dc20   89–15525
                                                                CIP

Titles in the Series

GENERAL EDITOR: GRAHAM BRADSHAW

General Editor's Preface

The *New Critical Introductions to Shakespeare* series will include studies of all Shakespeare's plays, together with two volumes on the non-dramatic verse, and is designed to offer a challenge to all students of Shakespeare.

Each volume will be brief enough to read in an evening, but long enough to avoid those constraints which are inevitable in articles and short essays. Each contributor will develop a sustained critical reading of the play in question, which addresses those difficulties and critical disagreements which each play has generated.

Different plays present different problems, different challenges and excitements. In isolating these, each volume will present a preliminary survey of the play's stage history and critical reception. The volumes then provide a more extended discussion of these matters in the main text, and of matters relating to genre, textual problems and the use of source material, or to historical and theoretical issues. But here, rather than setting a row of dragons at the gate, we have assumed that 'background' should figure only as it emerges into a critical foreground; part of the critical endeavour is to establish, and sift, those issues which seem most pressing.

So, for example, when Shakespeare determined that *his* Othello and Desdemona should have no time to live together, or that Cordelia dies while Hermione survives, his deliberate departures from his source material have a critical significance which is often blurred, when discussed in the context of lengthily detailed surveys of 'the sources'. Alternatively, plays like *The Merchant of Venice* or *Measure for Measure* show Shakespeare welding together different 'stories' from quite different sources, so that their relation to each other becomes a matter for critical debate. And Shakespeare's dramatic practice poses different critical questions when we ask – or if we ask: few do – why particular characters in a poetic drama speak only in verse or only in prose; or when we try to engage with those recent, dauntingly specialised and controversial textual studies which set out to establish the evidence for authorial revisions or joint authorship. We all read *King Lear* and *Macbeth*, but we are not all textual critics; nor are textual critics always able to show where their arguments have critical consequences which concern us all.

Just as we are not all textual critics, we are not all linguists, cultural anthropologists, psychoanalysts or New Historicists. The diversity of contemporary approaches to Shakespeare is unprecedented, enriching, bewildering. One aim of this series is to represent what is illuminating in this diversity. As the hastiest glance through the list of contributors will confirm, the series does not attempt to 'reread' Shakespeare by placing an ideological grid over the text and reporting on whatever shows through. Nor would the series' contributors always agree with each other's arguments, or premisses; but each has been invited to develop a sustained critical argument which will also provide its own critical and historical context – by taking account of those issues which have perplexed or divided audiences, readers, and critics past and present.

Graham Bradshaw

Contents

Preface

In rethinking *All's Well That Ends Well* I have tried to keep in mind the needs of audiences, readers and performers in order to write something helpful about the play – but not too helpful. There is a kind of essay that nannies the readers through a work line by line as if to preclude the disobedience of 'nuisance' questions. But finally, as in the morality play, Good Deeds must leave Everyman to his own experience. As audience, actor or reader of plays one soon learns that one's own experience is of prime importance since drama is the most open of literary forms, demanding collaboration to substantiate and complete the merely illusory finality of print.

To help resist some of the frailties of explanation I have considered the play by topic, rather than act by act. Inevitably there are blurred divisions and some overlaps in the discussions of 'sources', of affinities with the Sonnets, of the themes of status and sexuality, youth and age, and of the questions of dramaturgy that make up the chapters that follow. Not all scenes in the play are dealt with directly, yet some are discussed several times in different contexts. I make no apology for gaps and reconsiderations; they have the virtue of suggesting the tentativeness of interpretations and their openness to review. In addition, I have not always resisted the temptation of 'nuisance' questions – questions not strictly necessary to an understanding of *All's Well*, but the sort of question about, say, the relevance of source study or the logistics of Elizabethan dramaturgy that readers of the play inevitably bring to discussions of it.

In the course of the following chapters I have considered most if not all of the major critical issues that smoulder in learned debate. Since the First Folio of 1623 is the sole authority for the play and since its textual problems, though fairly numerous, do not often affect its meaning substantially, I have said little about textual matters. Otherwise the play as it emerges from modern criticism is consistently problematic: its heroine noble or vilely opportunist; its nominal hero a scoundrel, a young ass or a victim; its clowns witty and delightful or gross and offensive; its themes of love and war deeply plumbed or fudged; its ending joyous and exhilarating or tawdry and ironic – a Problem Play indeed! What follows touches on all such matters and on the attempts to resolve them by appeals to narrative tradition, production strategy and interpretative argument. The reader has been spared the awkwardness of extensive footnotes and elisions in quoted passages (all from G. K. Hunter's New Arden edition), both inappropriate to the tone and purpose of this work.

Sheldon Zitner

Acknowledgements

I am indebted to Alexander Leggatt for suggesting that I write this study, to Sue Roe and later Jackie Jones of Harvester Wheatsheaf for heroic patience and to Graham Bradshaw for that, for timely sympathy and for excellent advice. To my copy-editor I owe not only thanks but admiration. To my colleagues Nancy Lindheim and Brian Parker I owe useful insights and the encouragement of good example, and to David Hoeniger the benefit of his deep knowledge of Elizabethan medicine and of *All's Well*.

The Stage History

The title of *All's Well That Ends Well* seems prophetic of the play's fate in the theatre. Until three decades ago the stage history of *All's Well* made for short and simple annals indeed. Although the play was one of sixteen entered in the Stationers' Register by Blount and Jaggard in November, 1623 before they published the First Folio, its earliest recorded performance was at Henry Giffard's theatre in Goodman's Fields on 7 March, 1741. It was touted as a novelty, 'written by Shakespeare and not acted since his time', and its eight-performance run was a modest success. *All's Well* was chosen to lead off the following season, but William Millward, who played the King, died of a recurring respiratory disease and, when the run was resumed, Peg Woffington, his Helena, fainted in the wings and could not go on; hence the epithet 'unfortunate comedy' which has dogged the play ever since. Despite all this the play had ten performances. Apparently audiences were pleased by the comedy centring on Parolles, who was played by Theophilus Cibber. *All's Well* was revived in 1746, less successfully since Harry Woodward had to be substituted for Cibber on too short notice. Yet between 1741 and 1746 *All's Well* had been performed 22 times in four theatres. Joseph Price, whose *Unfortunate Comedy* (1968) is the authoritative study of the play's early stage history, informs us that this compares well

All's Well That Ends Well

with the runs of other comedies revived at the time.

Although there were some provincial productions of the play in the early 1750s, its next London revival was in 1756. The play was adapted, probably by Garrick, into a farcical vehicle for Parolles, who was played by Woodward, by now an accomplished comic actor. After further revision for a second performance, the adaptation had seven performances in all between 1756 and 1758. It was revived for two performances in 1762 at Drury Lane. A rival Covent Garden version was performed late in November of that year and after that occasionally (17 times in all) until 1774, the attraction once more being Woodward's Parolles.

All's Well was less successful in revivals by the brothers Kemble, John Philip late in 1794, and the younger Charles in 1811. John Kemble's adaptations, however, became the 'French's Acting Edition', used in London productions as late as 1852. Rejecting Garrick's emphasis on farce, Kemble transmogrified *All's Well* into sentimental comedy. Helena's selfless love dominated his 1811 version; gone were smut, bed-trick, ambition and ambiguity. Here was Coleridge's Romantic 'loveliest' Helena. Yet again the play was cursed: John Kemble fell ill during the production and hence was as '*merry* as a funeral'; Mrs Jordan as Helena was awkwardly pregnant in all five acts. The next performance, in 1811, with Charles Kemble as Bertram, was repeated only once. The play was produced at Covent Garden in 1832 as a kind of opera, and embellished with a masque, song and dance. Yet still it did not suit; it was insufficiently purged of a plot that was thought 'objectionable to modern refinement'. There was an eleven-night revival of the operatic version at Sadler's Wells in 1852, after which the play lay dormant for half a century, a silent tribute to Victorian high-mindedness. *All's Well* received only 17 performances during the nineteenth century, 11 of them as opera in 1852–3.

There were several attempts to rehabilitate the play after the First World War, largely in response to the needs of the Stratford-upon-Avon festivals. In 1916, 1922 and 1935 Benson, Bridges-Adams and Iden Payne offered productions, none of great interpretative distinction. There were some glimmers of a social rethinking of the play in William Poel's 1920 revival at the Ethical Church, Bayswater; the beginnings of a restoration of the play's 'indelicacies' in Robert Atkins's Old Vic production of 1921; and an attempt at balance between romance and realism in his third production of the play in 1940. However, the onset of the war (a performance was interrupted by air raids) dampened the play's comedy and seemed to move its plot toward melodrama.

The modern stage history, some would say *the* stage history, of the play properly begins with Tyrone Guthrie's Stratford, Ontario production in 1953 (1959 at Stratford-upon-Avon). The play was a grand success, with Irene Worth as Helena ('a rather more dangerous character to have around than Richard III', according to one reviewer), with greatly effective comic business and an exploration of the play's realism of motive and romanticism of plot, all of this placed in a handsome Edwardian setting designed by Tanya Moiseiwitsch. Since then the play has entered the flow if not the mainstream of the Shakespeare repertory. Critical laments that it is a stage failure, heard throughout the first half of the century (from Quiller-Couch in 1929 to Jay Halio in 1964) have given way first to surprised or grudging admissions that *All's Well* 'acts better than it reads', and then to the now widely shared certainty of its New Cambridge editor, Russell Fraser, that *All's Well* is a play whose time has come.

Among the productions that are both products and causes of this change of mind are Michael Benthall's fairy-tale production of 1953 for the Old Vic, with Claire Bloom as Helena, and John Barton's productions of 1967 and 1968 with their sensitivity and intelligence in realising the play's ironic observation of class and sexuality. Two subsequent productions deserve special notice, the first because it provided and still provides the most substantial audiences for the play. Elijah Moshinsky's elegant BBC *All's Well* offered all one could wish in conveying the profound intimacy between Angela Down's Helena and Celia Johnson's Countess, though some doubts have been expressed about Moshinsky's cutting, Donald Sinden's flamboyance as the King and the elevated sentiment of the last scene. Another distinguished recent production was Trevor Nunn's *All's Well* of 1981–2, with its sharp playing off of the romantic and the realistic, its surprisingly effective visual suggestions of World War I (both affirming the element of class friction in the play) and its nostalgic use of music and song. Harriet Walter's Helena and Peggy Ashcroft's Countess were deeply moving.

The excellence and diversity of productions in recent years is a just reward for the play's earlier paltry stage history. But plays performed often (as many of Shakespeare's plays are) sometimes ossify into acting or interpretative traditions, and these in turn call forth the challenge of useless high jinks. Ralph Berry records an interview with a Polish avant-garde director whose *All's Well* cast its leading males in a homosexual quadrille and had Lavatch utter his thoughtful follies while insinuating his hand up the Countess's skirt. For the most part, however, professional and amateur productions alike are still discovering the diversity of Shakespeare's 'unfortunate' comedy.

The Critical Reception

The critical reception of *All's Well* roughly parallels its stage history: an early silence; an apparent shift from appreciating the play as broad comedy in the later eighteenth century to preferring it as sentimental romance in the early nineteenth; then a disaffection from the play's supposed indecencies in Victorian times; and finally the two broad phases of twentieth-century response – earlier in the century efforts to define, deplore or explain away the play's supposed contradictions and defects and, since the Second World War, efforts to define and justify its ironies and achievements. Two obvious themes of this progression are the increasing specialisation and diffusion of criticism and the changing social ambience affecting critical opinion. The historicism of earlier twentieth-century criticism and the polarisation of views about Helena seem to reflect a strain of reductive causal thinking and the period's differing responses to the changing status of women. John Masefield's evaluation of Helena in *William Shakespeare* (1911) as 'a woman who practices a borrowed art, not for art's sake, not for charity, but, woman-fashion, for a selfish end' has a casual misogyny now mostly out of fashion. Less obviously and less dangerously regressive is Shaw's admiration for Helena as victim and embodiment of the Life Force. For a feminist like Katherine Mansfield, however, Helena was a

conventional horror. W. W. Lawrence's application of the
then current methods of folklore analysis (his article on
All's Well dates from 1922) seems now a by-product of
determinist historiography. The openness about sexuality,
the feminist critique and a pervasive disbelief in unmixed
motives, all themes of post-war thought, have opened up
the discussion of *All's Well* in directions not often taken
before.

Yet this neat series of stages requires some qualification.
Attitudes and arguments recur throughout the play's
critical history, and early on the more sophisticated critics
were aware of the ironies and contradictions celebrated in
the most recent discussions of the play. Dr Johnson's
famous inability to 'reconcile' himself to a Bertram who
is merely 'dismissed to happiness' suggests the dividedness
of both the play and his responses to it. And Coleridge's
phrase characterising 'loveliest' Helena is generally quoted
without reference to his strictures on the other side or his
shrewd defence of Bertram.

The attempt to rehabilitate the play began with W. W.
Lawrence's article and its appearance as a chapter of his
Shakespeare's Problem Comedies (1931). Lawrence argued
that the play should be understood in the light of its
'source-materials', popular tales that demand an invariable
response of sympathy to a Clever Wench who wins back
her husband – whatever the means. Yet this argument left
unresolved the inferences to be drawn from the differences
between *All's Well* and its far simpler antecedents. The
criticism of the 1950s was distinguished by further
influential attempts to come to grips with the play's
apparent anomalies, but now the anomalies were seen to
lie not in 'moral offenses' such as the bed-trick, but in
plot, character or ideas. For E. M. W. Tillyard, writing
in *Shakespeare's Problem Plays* (1949), the play failed
because of its want of energy in construction, style and
imagination, and this in turn arose from a failed attempt
to impose realism of motive on a romance plot. In the
same year Harold Wilson's *Huntington Library Quarterly*

article, 'Dramatic emphasis in *All's Well That Ends Well*', reached the opposite conclusion: not that Shakespeare had blundered into an impossible task but that he had deliberately and skilfully managed to avoid many of the pitfalls of this reconciliation of romance and reality, maintaining the audience's sympathy for Helena and its belief in Bertram's conversion. Earlier moral arguments against the play were radically overturned in Muriel Bradbrook's 'Virtue is the true nobility', a *Review of English Studies* article (also appearing in 1950) whose title summarises its view of the organising theme of the play. In addition to the theme, however, the play dramatised unrequited love in what seemed, according to Bradbrook, a return to the materials of the Sonnets. Clifford Leech's 'The theme of ambition in *All's Well That Ends Well*' (1954) and Albert H. Carter's 'In defence of Bertram' (1956) reflected an increasing willingness to recognise counter-tendencies in the play's characterisations. Leech argued for Shakespeare's deliberate departure from traditional values in Helena's intense and 'sick' determination to both love and control Bertram, and Carter for an acceptance of an element of justice in Bertram's attitudes as necessary to understanding Shakespeare's intention. At least equally significant was John Arthos's 'The comedy of generation' (1955), which saw the appreciation of the play as dependent on a detached perception of how its organising ideas on love, sexuality and procreation are worked out in the course of a narrative that Arthos believed was essentially optimistic. The criticism of the 1950s culminates in the thorough and perceptive introduction to G. K. Hunter's New Arden edition (1959), with its still influential argument that *All's Well* is a romance *manqué*, a play in which Shakespeare failed to solve the difficulty of dramatising reconciliation and forgiveness, a challenge that he finally mastered in his romances.

In the 1960s John F. Adams's '*All's Well That Ends Well:* the paradox of procreation' (1961), James L.

Calderwood's 'The mingled yarn of *All's Well*' (1963) and his 'Styles of knowing in *All's Well*' (1964) continued Arthos's focus on themes and ideas in the play, with Calderwood presenting some ingenious though arguable readings of the text. Also continued were the exploration of the ironies in the play's characterisations. Walter King's 1960 article 'Shakespeare's "mingled yarn"' attributes apparent anomalies of character to the play's psychological realism. A chapter of *Angel with Horns* (1961) by A. P. Rossiter, possibly the most congenial introduction to the play, also explores the priority of psychological realism over the moralism of the narrative. Robert Hapgood's 'The life of shame: Parolles and *All's Well*' (1965), a variation on this theme, explores the significance of the idea that Parolles, Helena, Bertram and others all are willing to risk dishonour in their hunger for love and for experience in general. In 'Chastity, regeneration and world order in *All's Well That Ends Well*' (1963), Eric La Guardia accepts the regeneration of Bertram as a *fait accompli*, and sees in Helena a redemptive religious purity. From this he generalises the play as an expression of optimism about the outcome of the perennial struggle against human corruptibility. Similar views had been advanced in 1958 in G. Wilson Knight's essay on the play in *The Sovereign Flower*. Knight's discussion of the element of miracle in *All's Well* has proved less interesting than his extended discussion of honour and less persuasive than his study of the play's language, an aspect of *All's Well* that has until recently, in such studies as Nicholas Brooke's '*All's Well That Ends Well*' for *Shakespeare Survey* (1977), been too readily treated as merely patchwork, a sign of Shakespeare's supposed inability to develop a 'style' for the play. Two other noteworthy articles of the 1960s exemplified the increasingly selective focus of scholarship. Robert Y. Turner's 'Dramatic conventions in *All's Well That Ends Well*' (1960) relates *All's Well* to the 'prodigal son' plays but discovers also significant departures from them. Roger Warren's 1969 *Shakespeare Survey* piece, 'Why does it end well? Helena, Bertram and the Sonnets', is a careful account of the relations between the play and the poems that goes on to speculate about the possible autobiographical element in the play. Two good thematic treatments of the play are the relevant chapter in R. G. Hunter's *Shakespeare and the Comedy of Forgiveness* (1965), and Jay Halio's 1964 essay in *Shakespeare Quarterly* pointing out the play's concern with old age, decline and death. Yet the indispensable achievement of the decade is Joseph G. Price's *The Unfortunate Comedy* (1968). Price has written an excellent stage and critical history of the play and provided a patient and humane survey of the major questions of genre, theme, character and dramatisation.

Criticism and scholarship during the later 1960s and the last two decades have been so extensive and varied as to demand a very selective topical presentation here. In addition to G. K. Hunter's Arden edition, the play has received almost uniformly excellent school editions with fine general introductions, among them the Pelican (Jonas Barish, 1964), the New Penguin (Barbara Everett, 1970) and the New Cambridge (Russell Fraser, 1985). All are challenging approaches to the play. The sources of the play are fully treated by Geoffrey Bullough in Volume 2 of *Narrative and Dramatic Sources of Shakespeare* (1958) and the development of the narrative material is informatively discussed by Howard Cole in *The 'All's Well' Story from Boccaccio to Shakespeare* (1981). The stage history and performance aspects of the play are the subject of J. L. Styan's indefatigable 1984 volume in the Manchester Press *Shakespeare in Performance* series and in the accounts of productions in *Shakespeare Survey* and *Shakespeare Quarterly*. Tyrone Guthrie in *A Life in the Theatre* (1959) and John Barton in an interview recorded in *Shakespeare Survey* (1972) are among the directors who have made useful comments on the play.

Interest in the play's social and political themes has been spurred by studies of Elizabethan class relations, best represented by the work of Lawrence Stone. Margaret L. Ranald's *Shakespeare and His Social Context* (1987) rehearses important materials on wardship and matrimonial law relevant to *All's Well*. Alexander Leggatt in '*All's Well That Ends Well:* the testing of romance' (1971) returns to the problem of the relation between romance and realism, seeing each as testing the other. In the course of his argument, he has some acute comments on the social world of the play and its ironic depiction of the military. The title of 'Though many of the rich are damn'd: dark comedy and social class in *All's Well That Ends Well*' (1977) summarises John Love's concerns in an article that sees Shakespeare's harsh depiction of class attitudes as undermining the themes of forgiveness and repentance.

Closely related to the rethinking of the play's representation of society are the numerous recent feminist studies. Marilyn Williamson's *The Patriarchy of Shakespeare's Comedies* (1986) and Juliet Dusinberre's *Shakespeare and the Nature of Women* (1975) suggest the variety and polarities of such studies, with Williamson offering not only a social paradigm of Shakespeare's comic forms but a significant treatment of wardship and its abuse, as well as perceptive observations on the implication for Shakespeare's comedies of the social exercise of power.

Almost as numerous are Freudian or Freudianising interpretations of the play. Arthur Kirsch in *Shakespeare and the Experience of Love* (1981) has a suggestive chapter combining psychoanalytic observation with a concern for the teachings of Pauline Christianity. Richard Wheeler's *Shakespeare's Development and the Problem Comedies: Turn and Counter-Turn* (1981) sees Helena as a representative of the dominant female, not only threatening but ambiguous. Less programmatic is Brian Parker's fine 1984 *Shakespeare Survey* article 'War and sex in *All's Well That Ends Well*'. Parker makes an acute analysis of male and female honour and sees the protagonists as led to abandon sterile ideals and develop the necessary qualities they lack for the possibility of love. Bertram must accept the responsibilities of sexuality and Helena the need for blunt self-assertion. A more conventional Freudian position is taken by Ruth Nevo in 'Motive and meaning in *All's Well That Ends Well*' (1987). Here Helena's problem is seen as the need 'to free her sexuality from the archaic bond of infancy . . .'. The criticism of the last two decades offers ample proof that *All's Well* now lays claim to an important place in discussions of Shakespeare's development – and his achievement.

· 1 ·

Fashioning the Story

As early as 1582 Stephen Gosson, a mediocre playwright turned anti-theatre pamphleteer, made the following complaint:

> I may boldly say it because I have seen it, that *The Palace of Pleasure*, *The Golden Ass*, *The Ethiopean History*, *Amadis of France*, the Round Table, bawdy Comedies in Latin, French, Italian, and Spanish, have been thoroughly ransacked to furnish the Play houses in London.

Gosson was primarily concerned with the moral damage caused by comedies that 'tickle the senses' and 'make us lovers of laughter'. His concern with literary quality was secondary, but he evidently found the classicising views of drama then fashionable congenial to his moral outrage. Like Sidney, who wrote his *Apology for Poetry* partly in reply to Gosson's attacks on the theatre, Gosson decried the drama's breaches of social and artistic decorum: its companioning of clowns with kings and its last-act marvels which reunited the far-travelled and long-lost through rings and handkerchiefs. If on nothing else, Gosson and Sidney agreed on the meretricious quality of early romantic comedy. Yet no critic, whether hostile or sympathetic to the theatre, would have raised seriously the most obvious modern objection to furnishing the stage with what Ben

Jonson was later to call 'mouldy tales'. Playwrights nowadays translate, modernise and adapt, but with some apology, and are typically more at ease in asserting that the germ of their play was a conversation overheard on a Philadelphia bus or ripped palpitating from their own experience. The idea of a play with a 'source' – with its *fons et origo* in someone else's twice-told tales – seems to deny the immediacy which is the theatre's special claim. The idea has seemed peculiar enough to strike some critics as perverse. F. W. Bateson suggested that Shakespeare borrowed the plots for his plays because 'he found human *action* of so little interest in itself' – an astounding notion in the face of what the plays actually give us! Yet its usefulness may well depend on how one defines *action*. One can take action to mean (as it does in, say, Aristotle's *Poetics*) the large arcs of overturn in human experience that provide the basic shapes of stories. A case can be made for action in this sense having relatively little intrinsic interest for the writer because the basic story shapes are relatively few and obvious in their recurrence. Aristotle advised playwrights to go on with what their predecessors had discovered was the best practice, that is, taking their *actions* from the limited number of central legends. After all, what the poet created was not this or that course of events but its significance. In any case, the central legends of the great families came to the Greeks already enriched with possibilities and likelihoods that would whet the audience's attention and enable the playwright to deepen their responses by outwitting their expectations. But Bateson's observation was probably meant to be provocative. If so it is ultimately an expression of the modern preference for 'realistic' bus conversations over mouldy tales. In point of fact, the economics of the theatre and the difficulties of its collective enterprise make the theatre as conservative as ever. It is still peculiarly an art of traditions, antecedents and spin-offs.

Understanding the idea of 'sources' is important for understanding the logistics of the Elizabethan theatrical imagination, and specifically useful for understanding *All's Well* since it can provide points of comparison that illuminate the dramatist's method and intent. Working through the idea of sources requires some historical retrievals, however. The whole notion looks suspiciously like a projection of the scholar's neat methods of academic essay-writing on to the improvisatory chaos of literary creation. Too often source study actually is the outcome of precisely such a projection. But as an enterprise source study is a creature of politics as well. As Oscar Cargill pointed out in *Intellectual America* (1968), source study became a central scholarly activity in early twentieth-century North American academic work as a borrowing from the practice of prestigious German universities and hence from the ideology of Pan-Germanism. The rediscovery of the Teutonic 'roots' of European civilisation as important alternatives to its traditional classical and Romance origins was a vindication of the German claim to the status of a seminal high culture. And the establishment of Germanic 'sources' for English literature echoed and reinforced the jockeying for imperial (especially British) alliance that preceded the First World War. In addition, source study was a step in 'scientising' literary scholarship by bringing its documents into a causal scheme and so rendering it respectable as a 'modern' study. Such social and political biases prejudiced, and in some cases still do, more sophisticated views of the relations between playwrights and their literary antecedents.

The veneration of precedent, the distrust of individual imagination, the wariness of the new – now the traits of troglodyte literary minorities – were pervasive common-places in the early seventeenth century, attitudes variously reflected in Shakespeare's respectful treatment of the medieval poet Gower in *The Winter's Tale*, in his constant (though sometimes mischievous) use of proverbs and in lines like 'So all my best is dressing old words new', which offer a complimentary defence of the sonnet-poet's avoidance of 'new-found methods'. Shakespeare did not

go as far as Chaucer, who invented a Lollius, the fictitious
source of his *Troilus and Criseyde*, but, as did Joyce in
Ulysses, he no doubt recognised the uses of a time-
winnowed story, with its authoritativeness and freedom
from the merely contemporary, the parochial and the
eccentric, all too common in 'original' contrivances. A
great task of sixteenth- and seventeenth-century story-
tellers, as William Nelson points out in *Fact or Fiction:
the Dilemma of the Renaissance Storyteller* (1973), was to
justify fictional narrative as having a credibility and truth-
value like that of history. Here the authoritativeness of
old precedents was invaluable.

There were simpler, economic reasons for dependence
on 'sources' in the early 1600s. The theatres had only in
the last two decades become fairly profitable, if still not
easily predictable, economic enterprises. A company could
minimise its risks and best utilise its resources by producing
plays based on materials that had succeeded before: hence
the attractiveness of stock characters and familiar situations.
The sources of narrative listed by Gosson provided an
anthology of popular motifs and character-types, and,
above all, ways of conventionalising experience that could
serve as templates for dramatic composition. To group
Shakespeare's comedies by mood and structure, as Salingar
(p. 299) points out, is to group them by sources.

Medieval romances were even more out of favour in
the early 1600s than they had been when Gosson
and Sidney condemned them twenty years before. Yet
Shakespeare did not turn his back on their motifs of
prolonged trials, the division and reintegration of families,
or on their heroines – especially persecuted wives – who
endured danger and suffering for the sake of love. (There
was no vogue for stories about accused husbands.)
The classical comedies of Plautus and Terence offered
Elizabethan playwrights effective techniques for construction, among them the introduction of variations from the
chronology of events so as to clarify the causal connections
among the incidents. These in turn permitted more fully

conceived characters, and allowed for the pleasures of dramatic irony and ingenious intrigue. The plots of classical New Comedy, with their wandering protagonists and their climaxes involving questions of paternity, provided materials for *The Ethiopian History* of Heliodorus, which Gosson mentions, and ultimately also for the Italian *novelle* whose plots Shakespeare used. So understood, much of the European narrative tradition becomes a 'source' for the plays. The critical task is less to identify 'sources' than to specify what the dramatist did with his inheritance.

The immediate narrative antecedent of *All's Well* was Boccaccio's brief story of Giletta and Beltramo in the *Decameron*. Shakespeare might possibly have had enough Italian (he was familiar with the dictionary-texts of John Florio) to consult the tale in the original. It is more likely that he used the French translation of Antoine le Maçon, but very probable that he knew the close English translation in William Painter's extremely popular collection *The Palace of Pleasure* (1566–7, 1575).

Boccaccio's story of Giletta and Beltramo is the ninth told on the third day of the *Decameron*. A group of young aristocrats has gone into the countryside to escape the plague in Florence. They decide to pass the time pleasantly by telling stories on a theme that they change from day to day. The theme of the third day is the variability of Fortune, especially as it affects those who 'have acquired, by their diligence, something greatly wanted by them, or else recovered what they had lost'. In Boccaccio's story, Isnardo, the Count of Rossiglione, who was 'sickly and diseased', kept a house physician, Gerardo of Narbona, whose daughter Giletta had been brought up with the Count's only son, the 'amiable and fayre' Beltramo. Giletta fell in love with the boy 'more then was meete for a maiden of her age'. At the Count's death Beltramo was placed in the custody of the King and sent off to Paris, leaving Giletta 'very pensife'. Shortly after, Giletta too was orphaned, and wanted to follow

Beltramo to Paris. Since she was now wealthy and fatherless her relatives attempted to marry her off, but she 'refused manye husbands'. Hearing of the King's fistula, she set off to Paris with 'a pouder of certaine herbes' she had learned from her father and, after visiting Beltramo, offered to allow herself to be burnt at the stake if she did not cure the King in eight days, with God's help. As a reward the King offered to find her a husband; she proposed that he be a husband of her choosing, with the royal line excepted from her choice. The King is cured but is 'very loth to graunt' her choice of Count Beltramo, yet even more reluctant to break his promise. For his part, although Beltramo knows Giletta to be fair, she is not 'of a stock convenable to his nobility', and hence unacceptable to him. Despite Beltramo's scornful protests that he will never be contented with the marriage, it takes place.

Beltramo is granted leave to consummate the marriage in Rossiglione, but once on horseback he rides off to Tuscany to join Florence in its war against Siena. Once there, he is 'made captaine of a certain number of men'. Giletta goes to Rossiglione, where she proceeds to organise the Count's estates and win the affection of his subjects, even restoring again 'their auncient liberties'. This done she sends word to Beltramo that if he had gone into exile because of her, 'she to do him pleasure would departe from thence'. His 'chorlish' reply was that only if she could get his 'greatly loved ring', which had 'a certaine vertue', and beget a son by him would he consent to live with her.

On receiving this message Giletta 'assembled the noblest and chiefest of her Countrie' and told them that rather than keep Beltramo in exile she would leave them in charge of the estates and go on perpetual pilgrimage. Yet her purpose, fulfilling the impossible tasks, was clear.

Taking off with a small party and a considerable amount of silver and precious jewels, Giletta travelled rapidly to Florence. Hearing of Beltramo's love for an impoverished

young woman, she offers to provide the girl with a dowry
if her mother will get Beltramo's ring, and if the young
woman herself will agree to meet him, but allow Giletta
to take her place in bed. The plot prospers. After 'manye'
assignations and gifts from Beltramo, Giletta has the ring,
and is pregnant with 'two goodly sons'. Giletta overcomes
the polite reluctance of her benefactors, rewards them
richly, and returns to Rossiglione after delivering the
twins and hearing that her husband has arrived home. She
times her own arrival to coincide with a great feast,
declares to the assembly that she has accomplished the
tasks set by her husband, and presents the evidence.
Beltramo, astonished at her story, considers her 'constant
minde and good witte, and twoo faire young boyes' and
the opinions of the assembly. He then 'abjected his
obstinate rigour' and loved and honoured her thereafter.

The story of Giletta and Beltramo is recognisable in the
plot of *All's Well*, but in almost every respect – detail and
emphasis of the incidents, depth and motivation of
the characters, social ambience and setting, moral and
intellectual ethos – the story and the play are unlike. In
addition to extensive alterations, Shakespeare has added
major and minor characters, excised others, introduced a
subplot and substituted an ending radically different in
incident and effect. Indeed, so much is changed that it
seems necessary to ask what could have attracted Shakespeare to the Boccaccio story in the first place.

Tales of persecuted wives and of women enduring
hardships for love were extremely popular in Shakespeare's
day and had been so for centuries. The reasons for this
popularity seem to be largely sociological, although the
attractiveness of survival stories is, for obvious reasons,
universal. Tales of persecuted women provided models of
fidelity and submissiveness, thus reinforcing the idea of
male dominance by appearing to legitimise it. And by
insisting on the reality of women's suffering and their
freedom from guilt, the stories offered occasions for
specious male sympathy that prompted no ameliorating

action since the accused were vindicated and the long-
suffering rewarded. The stories of persecuted women were
the obverse of the misogynist story of Eve and the serpent
yet, viewed as social instruments, their effect could be
essentially the same. As the extreme of the type, the
patient Griselda story was long an international favourite.
No doubt women were educated to draw from these plots
some lean comfort. Whether because of economic prudence
or a temperament in tune with his audience, Shakespeare
was attracted to such stories, as is obvious from plays as
far apart as *Two Gentlemen of Verona* and *The Winter's
Tale*. Needless to say, Shakespeare's treatment of the
stories deflected many of their ideological implications.
The theme of woman suffering and vindicated is a variation
on two other popular motifs that attracted the playwright:
prolonged trials by circumstance, and families first divided,
then reconciled.

A later chapter will treat in detail some of the intellectual
attractions of such stories as Giletta's. Here it is convenient
to note an important point of agreement between Shakespeare and Boccaccio. For both, love was an intractable
and vitalising force. Helena's soliloquy at the end of the
first scene of *All's Well* is one of many tributes in both
Shakespeare and Boccaccio to the power of love and to
its capacity to transform those it strikes – especially
women – by granting them wit, initiative, and courage.
'Who ever strove/To show her merit that did miss her
love?' Here Helena is only echoing the many passages in
the *Decameron* in which love brooks neither advice nor
opposition, and inspires women with the wit and courage
for successful intrigues and strategies taught by neither
poets or philosophers. For Shakespeare as for Boccaccio
love was the great means; its great end was itself fulfilled,
love requited.

Boccaccio's hedonistic naturalism provided Shakespeare
with a congenial context in which to create the witty and
ingenious women of his comedies. Not, of course, that
Shakespeare needed Boccaccio for what experience and

reflection had evidently provided in the first place. Shakespeare has few patient Griseldas in his plays, none of them major figures, and not only because the Elizabethan stage was an odd place for passivity. When he personifies Patience, Shakespeare puts her on a monument.

The force of love in Boccaccio's Giletta story is exerted in the performance of impossible tasks required to bridge a great social distance. Besides the technical convenience of providing at the outset of the play the visible terminal point needed in play construction, the Giletta plot allowed Shakespeare to deal with another of his recurring themes, the place of merit in a world of privilege. In *All's Well* as in his other plays, Shakespeare's sources, whatever their qualities or the particular details of their attraction, seem to have marshalled the playwright the way that he was going.

The most obvious change that Shakespeare makes in the Boccaccio story is a radical transformation of its ethos, the outlook from which the story is told. In Boccaccio the story turns on Giletta's persistence and ingenuity in getting Beltramo to face and accept the realities of his situation. The chief of these is the power of Love, which is totally on Giletta's side. The ring and the twin sons are proof of this reality. The second reality is the undeniable appropriateness of the match, an appropriateness that Giletta has demonstrated despite time, distance, prejudice and material obstacles. She has taken the estate Beltramo left in confusion and, good bourgeoise that she is, has set it to turning a profit. Beltramo's tenants love her, and in a piece of daring that could hardly have been an idea the Count would have thought of though he must have seen its practicality when in force, Giletta restored the ancient liberties to the countryside. Her Florentine intrigue is brilliantly efficient and decorously managed. Furthermore, Giletta chooses a great public feast for her return. This forces Beltramo's hand. Dare he be mean-spirited enough to reject this local, living saint on All Saint's Day, and before a partisan crowd? Giletta not only traps Beltramo graciously, but – on her knees – gives him a wondrous occasion to rise to. In any case, Beltramo, unlike Bertram, is not only 'fayre' but amiable. He had also grown up with Giletta; she was a quantity now fully known, and she had behaved admirably. Further, she was rich and had the skills, among them a store of nostrums, to play the perfect chatelaine. It is only midway in the story that Boccaccio thinks to tell us that she is fair. Like the mother of the unmarried gentlewoman of the bed-trick, Beltramo and everyone else in the *Decamaron* tale can think of 'nothing in the world whereof [to be] more desirous, than honest comfort'.

Not wealth, power, courage, honour, virtue, merit and all the other high and low abstractions so much in question in *All's Well* concern Boccaccio, but 'honest comfort' – physical ease, an ease which seems to value honesty and the other virtues primarily as qualities whose absence would make for discomfort. This is the perspective from which Beltramo seems to have seen the mismatch the King imposes on him. 'I shal never be contented with that mariage.' The King counters by predicting that life with Giletta will be 'more joyful . . . with her, then with a Lady of greater house'. This ends the debate. Contentment and comfort appear again as measures of events. Giletta is 'scarce contented' with her husband's unkindness, and Beltramo's subjects, after coming to know Giletta, blame the Count 'because he could not content himself with her'. She proposes the bed-trick to the gentlewoman as something that will 'both comfort me and your selfe' and afterwards refers to it with 'pleasure'; the narrator also states that the gentlewoman 'not onely contented the Countesse at that time, with the companye of her husbande, but at manye other times . . .'. *All's Well*-type morality-questions are irrelevant.

The wish for honest comfort is the most democratic of desires – the small somewhere of Liza Doolittle's yearning. It makes the matter of class distinction far less formidable than it becomes in *All's Well*. Boccaccio's people are

decent folk, thoroughly mature, and of superbly ordinary
sensibilities. Boccaccio himself – like them – moralizes
nothing, symbolises nothing, treats nothing as matter for
anguished self-division. Beltramo's affair with the nameless
young gentlewoman is no occasion for apostrophe,
reflection or platitude. She is nameless (no 'Diana' to set
moral reverberations buzzing). Her mother tells Giletta
that although she doesn't know the Count to be in love
(the word is hers) with her daughter, 'the likelyhood is
greater', and the mother's only concern is the practical
one of safeguarding the young woman's reputation.
Neither the mother nor Giletta has anything unkind to
say about Beltramo. The occasion is one for practical
sisterly solidarity only.

In the Giletta story there is only one ring, and far from
symbolising anything like the royal debt owed to Helena,
or Bertram's family honour, Beltramo's ring is something
he covets only because it has 'a certain vertue'. Giletta,
unlike Helena, does not sleep with her husband only
once. Her pregnancy thus does not hint at the intervention
of providence or destiny. It is merely statistically more
likely. That she conceives twins is as close to the symbolic
as Boccaccio comes, but is less a symbol than an intensifier.

Giletta pursues her task in a thoroughly businesslike
manner. Her reflections are pragmatic thoughts and wishes
of the same generation. When Giletta heard that the King
'like one in dispaire would take no counsell or helpe',
'the young mayden was wonderfull glad', thinking this
the opportunity for a trip to Paris and a chance to see
Beltramo. She has no problems with her ambition (the
question never arises), nor with moral introspection. Her
cure is 'a pouder of certaine herbes' rather than the
unfathomable business of *All's Well*, and though both she
and the King also invoke the name of the Lord, there is
no *All's Well* hocus-pocus about it, nor any overtone of
the idea of the medical efficacy of virgin practitioners.
Giletta is indeed the model practical opportunist. As is
not the case in *All's Well*, it is the King who suggests that

he will provide a husband. Giletta takes the cue and asks for the right to choose. This the King 'incontinently' grants.

The *Decameron* story moves swiftly and unreflectively, its characters hardly more than a capacity for their roles, leaving generalisation or moral reflection almost entirely up to the reader, who in any case has been positioned for passive enjoyment if only by the rubric of the Third Day, the opening summary of the story which focuses attention on the intrigue, and by its rapid unfolding. The ethos of the tale is a self-consistent matter-of-factness whose ideas are in things, and whose appearances are its realities. Even Giletta's infatuation is naturalised to this reasonableness; it is merely 'more than was meete' at her age, understandable as a 'natural' result of childhood association, its breach of class differences mitigated in part by common upbringing. Beltramo's departure for Paris leaves her only 'pensife'. Through the displeasure of the King and the authorial adverb 'incontinently' applied to the King's agreement to Giletta's request, Boccaccio makes it clear that Giletta has violated the social code. So has Beltramo in his 'chorlish' reply. Though no one but Bertram seems scandalised in *All's Well*, much more of an issue is made of the social violation in the play than in the story. Helena's poverty and lack of family connections, even the discussion of status and virtue, emphasise the gap in fortune, which in Boccaccio is all but absorbed in the focus on the primacy of love and the rapidity of incident. In Boccaccio the King's praise of Giletta is a small rationalisation of his commitment, not part of a philosophic set-speech.

Despite Shakespeare's obvious sympathies with Boccaccian naturalism, he was not content with the reasonable world of *Decameron* story, whose only unreasonable element, its activating impulse, was love, albeit love cleared of the ambiguities arising from social custom of individual psychology. These Boccaccio simply externalised, making them obstacles which love easily removed. Shakespeare transferred the *Decameron* story from sunlight into shadow, not abandoning Boccaccio's naturalism, but making it problematic, turning its social and sexual givens into occasions for moral reflection and private anguish. As a result, character and motive become contradictory, and standards of judgement other than the right and natural claims of love make ironic and questionable the implications of the original. Yet as in the other 'problem' comedies, Shakespeare did not reduce the Giletta story to irony wholly unrelieved. In *Measure for Measure* the old judge Escalus speaks for a reasonable if often thwarted humane administration of justice. In *Troilus* Hector's exposure of the impulsive relativism for which Troilus argues offers an obvious ground for the rejection of time's distortions and disvaluations of love and honour – even for Hector's rejection of his own position. In *All's Well*, however, reassurance is at once less intellectual, more pervasive and more subtle; it is embodied in the nurturing bond between generations rather than dependent on individual wisdom of philosophic positions. Shakespeare's most striking alteration of Boccaccio's story is the invention of a senior generation for which there is little or no warrant in the original. The Countess and Lafew are wholly Shakespeare's invention; the King a radical expansion and rethinking of Boccaccio, and the Widow a fusion and fleshing out of two rather slight figures in the *Decameron*. Recollections of Helena's father and Beltramo's solidify the impression Shakespeare is imagining. Each of the elders acts to some degree as sponsor and protector of one, sometimes two, members of the younger generation: Bertram is the ward of the King whose hopes of him derive from memories of his father. His mother charges Lafew with Bertram's care at court. The Countess adopts Helena, Lafew befriends her; the King rewards the cure made possible by her father's art, and the Widow aids her in fulfilling the other impossible tasks. In addition, the Widow protects her own daughter, and the King offers to procure a husband for Diana, despite the unhappy outcome of his last such offer. Finally, in the face of all he knows and all that his protégé is, Lafew determines to protect Parolles. Parolles' famous 'Simply the thing I am shall make me live', in which he suppresses his confidence that, 'being fooled', he can 'by foolery thrive', proves less accurate than a second assertion, that 'There's place and means for every man alive'. This second statement seems to make survival depend on a kindly divine dispensation, and more immediately on the human charity which is evidence of it.

The relation between the arbitrary, often ineffectual, yet always anxious nurturing of the elders and the impulsive wrong-headedness, obsession and chicanery of the young is an anagram of New Comedy construction. Far from being rival blocking figures, the old encourage romance; the clever servant-figure turns out, in the case of Parolles, to be a fool; in the case of Helena to be a victorious protagonist; and only in the case of Lavatch to approach the traditional role of go-between and ironic observer.

These differences in ethos and construction between play and 'source' should discourage both the literal interpretation of that word and any agreement with Bateson's notion of a Shakespeare turning to sources out of a lack of interest in human action. It should also make one sceptical of the reductive interpretations of critics who extract from both the story and the play folklore materials that supposedly carry with them imperatives for response. Roughly, the argument is that the basic motifs of *All's Well* are the success of a Clever Wench engaged first in Healing the King and then in the Fulfilment of Impossible Tasks. In folk-tale these motifs are always expected to elicit the same response of benign approval. Thus it is argued that there can be no proper basis for questioning, let alone feeling revulsion at, the bed-trick, or for seeing anything negative or even problematic in Helena's 'ambition' or her inner anguish. A Clever Wench is always to be approved when she is performing Impossible Tasks.

Nor is there much point in disgust with Bertram. His cold ingenuity is simply a requirement of the motifs: the harder the taskmaster, the more nearly Impossible the Tasks. Finally, once the Impossibility is surmounted and the Clever Wench gains her goal it is beside the point to question her happiness (she has earned it), or to stick at doubts about whether the taskmaster has reformed or has been forgiven. Much scholarly work has gone into articulating such views. But the line of argument seems weak on several counts. It assumes an inevitable and unchanging correspondence between motifs and meanings – emotional meanings among others – and thus that the author's hands are tied by the materials he chooses. But in fictions the whole is not even the sum of all, let alone a few, of its parts. In any case, how far *All's Well* is from the relative simplicities of folk-tale is apparent from its psychological complexity. Helena is clever in ways beyond those of the Clever Wench, whose cleverness consists only in narrowly pursuing her ends, not in the 'cleverness' apparent in Helena's understanding of Parolles, or her perceptive self-division, or in her seeing (and feeling) the moral contradictions of the bed-trick, or in devising the elaborate charades of Act 5, most of them unnecessary for a folklorish conclusion, which would not have equivocated on the matter of a happy ending. A folktale Lafew would have smelled roses, not onions. The play's distance from folk-tale is also apparent in the thematic complexity of its social ambience. Issues of war, peace and diplomatic alliance are handled with a critical alertness absent from Boccaccio or his antecedents; issues of sexuality and status with a questioning seriousness that treats them as more than mere barriers to be breached by Clever Wenches. The traditional wisdom of the folk can be shrewd and unsparing, yet it is by nature conservative. Whatever conclusions one wants to draw from them, the social and psychological perceptions of *All's Well* are not.

Errors in critical thinking can too easily be encouraged by the mechanical use of indexes of folklore motifs. Bits of narrative incident or of character and motif do not prompt unchanging responses when transferred from context to context any more than colours do. *All's Well* offers its own clues for its decoding to reader and audience. There is no need for a royal road of interpretation that derives the significance of *All's Well* from Boccaccio, let alone the folk-tale sources of the source. But comparisons have their uses; to follow the many differences between *All's Well* and Boccaccio's story is to step inside the poet's workshop.

Several obvious alterations Shakespeare makes are usually attributed to necessary theatrical compression. For example, he reduces the time over which Giletta's story takes place. In Painter and Boccaccio Beltramo's father dies and the boy is sent off to Paris. '[A] little while after', Giletta's father dies. She is kept from following Beltramo for some years. In the interim, Beltramo has become a young man and Giletta has had time to fend off her relatives' matchmaking and many offers of marriage. The cure of the King takes place within two, rather than eight, days. Giletta spends enough time at Rossiglione to reorganise the estates, Helena almost none at all, and she lies with Bertram one rather than Giletta's many nights with the unwitting Beltramo. In each case, however, the compression is not only a tightening of plot, but imposes a significant change on the import of the basic story material. By placing the deaths of both parents close together, Shakespeare makes Helena's falling in love with Bertram a passion of youth rather than an extension of childhood proximity; she falls in love with a young man rather than childishly with a playmate. Moreover, the nearness of the deaths of the two parents makes their children's parallel 'wardship' more apparent and so emphasises the radical mismatch in intellectual depth and maturity. Finally, placing together the deaths of both fathers offers the occasion for Helena's guilt at sighing for a departing lover rather than mourning for a dead parent and so initiates the themes of her inwardness and scruple. Eliminating Giletta's period of fending off suitors, like the elimination of Giletta's success as chatelaine of Rossiglione, is a way of widening the social differences between Helena and Bertram. Helena, poor and subservient, is a much less likely match for a nobleman than is Giletta, rich, sought-after and managerial. Even Giletta's visit to Beltramo in Paris before she sees the King suggests again her relative social and personal acceptability. Giletta's clarity about her motives and plans at every point is dispelled in Shakespeare, making Helena a far more inward, problematic character. Eliminating the long, active stay at Rossiglione also focuses on the inwardness of Helena and on her eloquent self-examination. The same effect follows from the remarkable rapidity of the cure. Two days suggests a providential wonder drug; eight days a cure such as nature – with ordinary medical help – might effect. The impression left by this rapidity is reinforced by the relative vagueness of the 'dearest issue' of Helena's father's practice as compared to Giletta's herbal remedy, which is presented as matter-of-fact in matter-of-fact prose rather than in the mysticising couplets of the play.

If Shakespeare compresses the time-span of Boccaccio's story he is at least as generous as Boccaccio in his treatment of space. *All's Well* is a tale of an estate and three cities: Rossillion, Paris, Florence and Marseilles; in addition, Parolles is exposed as a coward somewhere outside the camp in the Tuscan countryside. This violation of the so-called Aristotelian unity of place was typical of romantic plays and much decried by classicising critics like Sidney and after him Ben Jonson. The 'rule' of single place does not seem to have impressed Shakespeare. While deromanticising Boccaccio's story, he emphasises the numerous changes of scene that were a hallmark of romantic drama, sharpening the disparity between the romantic genre and the realistic tone that distinguishes *All's Well*, a comedy Shaw might well have classified as a Play Unpleasant. From the first it is obvious that Giletta will achieve her goal, not only to cure the King and marry

Beltramo, but to live with him 'in great honour and felicity'. The summary preceding the story tells us so, even if we have forgotten the rubric for the *Decameron*'s Third Day, which calls for stories of those who achieve or regain a desired state. Boccaccio's tale is a straight road from desire to fulfilment. In the play, character, motive and incident are so managed as to make the last and most important of Helena's three goals – living happily with Bertram – not only highly unlikely but possibly even perverse. Shakespeare works to divert the course of the *Decameron* story. The tale of Giletta and Beltramo exemplifies Boccaccio's outlook in its focus on the intractability and single-mindedness of sexual passion. Yet the tale of Giletta and Beltramo is also romantic. It insists on a larger appropriateness in the pairing off of its protagonists and on their mutual worthiness and deserving. In romance, Beauty may couple with a Beast, but only with a prince of frogs. To marry a real frog may be more common, but it is not romance. Boccaccio's ironies and harshness are reserved for love's enemies and failures, not for love's successes.

The series of alterations some critics think designed to blacken Bertram and raise Helena in our eyes does so inconsistently. The alterations seem more consistently directed toward denying the romantic ethos of the source and making its ending seem problematic or ironic. The denigration of Bertram is fairly thorough, however. Shakespeare's King is gentler than is Boccaccio's King to Beltramo in announcing his decision on the match, and he argues for it more eloquently. In Shakespeare other noble bachelors seem eager to comply and marry Helena; Bertram's reaction is thus made to seem more blameworthy than is Beltramo's. Beltramo is, in any case, a mature figure apparently ready for a 'convenable' marriage, hardly the petulant naïf unready for any genuine intimacy but eager enough to run off to the wars. For Bertram a young man married is a man that's marred. But the immaturity that partly excuses Bertram still leaves him a figure inappropriate for the romantic ending since he seems even then not to have grown up. He is perhaps sadder and wiser for knowing Parolles' duplicity, but apparently neither wiser nor sadder for having others know his own. Successful military service has done nothing for his character but given him a rationalising metaphor (conquest) for seduction. Again, Beltramo imposes the impossible tasks on Giletta out of what seems sudden pique; they are a churlish reply to Giletta's message offering to leave Rossiglione if indeed she is the cause of his exile. Bertram, unlike Beltramo, lacks the courage to face the King and ask leave to return to his estates. He begs by surrogate and letter. Worse again than Beltramo's spoken annoyance are Bertram's instructions on the impossible tasks. They are written in cold blood almost immediately after the marriage. Bertram's fifth-act marathon of lies and evasions contrasts with Beltramo's good-natured rationality in finally accepting Giletta. Bertram's positive nastiness and the extenuations of it in his lack of 'seasoning' and his oppressive subjection by the King create a complex, unpleasant and questionably redeemable figure. Yet one wonders whether it is fair to anyone, even a Bertram, to make his acceptance of an imposed marriage the mark of his maturity. To further darken the picture, this callow young man is dismayingly successful as a warrior.

Helena, better and worse than her predecessor, is also not quite the proper *ingénue* for a romance conclusion. As with Bertram, her particular psychological complexity may well unfit her for this particular romance. In the Boccaccio story sexuality lies immediately beneath the verbal surface, a generating force, acted out rather than discussed, its physical side typically veiled by euphemism or by the verbal sleight that assimilates sexual satisfaction to the omnipresent 'content'. Presumably, though, if Giletta's love for Beltramo was more than 'meete' for her years, one can assume a time of life when such intensity might have been appropriate, perhaps even too little. In part, Boccaccio's reticence reflects his period's particular

linguistic temper. Whatever the case, in *All's Well* the
language of physical sexuality is more than Elizabethan
verbal ebullience; it is deliberately blunt and open in
Parolles' and Helena's exchange on virginity, in Lavatch's
coarseness, in Diana's revulsion and in Helena's wondering
reaction after the bed-trick. In the very first speech of the
play, the Countess's word 'delivering' for her transfer of
her son to wardship and her husband-son equation provide
evidence of Shakespeare's understanding of what can lurk
in the psychic depths. And there is a significant difference
between Giletta's falling in love and wanting to marry
Beltramo and Helena's wanting to lose her virginity to
her own liking.

Overt discussion of it pits the erotic side of Helena's
love against both its implied ideal side and against Helena's
sense of shame and impropriety; to say nothing of pitting
it against the views of high-minded male critics who find
this three-dimensional Helena hypocritical or at best self-
deceiving. Giletta's unreflective directness escapes such
strictures. For some critics, ambition – the word is
Helena's – also devalues her love. There is no question
of Helena's being motivated only by Bertram's wealth and
station, but she inflicts all the mean connotations of the
word on herself none the less. Her self-dramatising guilt
at scanting grief for her dead father while shedding 'great
tears' at Bertram's departure; her sense of having betrayed
her benefactor, the Countess, by falling in love with the
Countess's son; her later embarrassment and retreat at
court after Bertram's expression of reluctance; her guilty
fears for Bertram's safety in the Florentine wars complete
the psychological complexity imposed on Boccaccio's
single-minded agent of love. Helena has become a focus
for all the considerations of station, occasion and scruple
whose easy overthrow in Boccaccio went to demonstrate
love's irresistible force. Helena's progress toward her goals
is marked by self-questioning, no doubt a tribute to her
character. But the failure to follow Boccaccio in making
clear from the outset that in undertaking her pilgrimage

she has resolved .to satisfy Bertram's terms, rather than
validating this character, seems at times to call it into
question and to make her inwardness and doubts only
strategies. One may argue that Helena is the victim of a
society that does not permit her a 'male' freedom, and
that she must seem passive if she is to balance the daring
of her choice with conventional submissiveness. The
argument is just, but is it asserted strongly enough in the
play to prevent a clouding of her motives? And the
exquisitely painful, drawn-out contrivance of Bertram's
exposure, while self-justifying as theatre, cannot help
making Helena seem even more problematic. That Helena
persists in loving Bertram despite everything confirms the
playwright's agreement in one respect with the spirit of
his source. Love is perhaps even more of an intractable
force in the play than in the story since love overcomes
not only external obstacles but real self-doubts, which
Giletta lacks entirely. Yet Boccaccio's simple romance
seems at times to sink under Shakespeare's revision.

If Shakespeare makes his Helena and Bertram inappropriate for a Boccaccian conclusion, he makes the intellectual
and social ambience of *All's Well* even less accommodating
to the tale. Abstract ideas of merit and moral action do
not become issues in the Giletta story. In *All's Well*, they
do. The complications of motive and action that distance
Helena and Bertram from Giletta and Beltramo generate
the troubling ideas of status and sexuality discussed in the
play. Moreover, in the *Decameron* tale the ambience,
whether Rossiglione, Paris or Florence, is a thinly painted
cloth against which events occur without much reference
to their setting. Meaning lies almost exclusively in the
events themselves. *All's Well*, however, insists on a causal
rather than a happenstance connection of place with event.
The curious diplomatic relation between Paris and Florence
defines the war to which Bertram commits himself and
so defines both the limited nature of the King's power
and the emptiness of Bertram's commitment. The war is
not, as it is to Beltramo, merely some place other than

Rossiglione. The household at Rossillion and the Paris court provide measures of style and aspiration against which Helena and Bertram are defined. Nor are Shakespeare's additions, the older generation and Lavatch and Parolles, merely by the by comic relief. Each helps to clarify issues that Boccaccio's story leaves unraised, issues that in turn define the particular tone and import of *All's Well*.

Among these issues are sexuality and status, about which the play says much and implies more. When Shakespeare came to write *All's Well* he had already worked out much of his thinking on these matters in the Sonnets, inevitably a more immediate, personal form than the drama. In that sense, Shakespeare was his own source for much of *All's Well*.

· 2 ·

In the Sonnet Workshop

Connections between *All's Well* and the Sonnets have been pointed out before. Muriel Bradbrook (*RES*, XXVI, 1950) observed that in *All's Well* 'the juxtaposition of the social problem of high birth versus native merit and the human problem of unrequited love recalls the story of the Sonnets; the speeches of Helena contain echoes of the Sonnets [and] the way in which Bertram is condemned recalls also the plain speaking which is so unusual a feature of the Sonnets'. The violence of Helena's language in her soliloquy at the end of III. ii. reminds Roger Warren, who has written most extensively on the relation between the poems and the play (*SS*, 22, 1969, pp. 79–92), of several sonnets – 88 and 92 among them. Her 'abject devotion', Warren adds, echoes sonnets 57 and 58. Other commentators on the Sonnets, among them Walter Lever (*The Elizabethan Love Sonnet*, 1956, p. 185) and J. B. Leishman (*Themes and Variations*, 1963, p. 33), have pointed out the similarities between the 'religiously idolatrous' love of sonnets like 31 and Helena's feelings for Bertram, or the parallel between 'Shakespeare's extreme capacity for self-effacement' in sonnets 57 and 87 and, say, Helena's brief speech as she chooses Bertram in II. iii. Equally suggestive are the observations in John Kerrigan's introduction to his 1986 edition of *The Sonnets and A Lover's Complaint*. The contrast Kerrigan develops

23

between the Dark Lady and the still-loving lover of the *Complaint*, like the contrast between the Dark Lady and the *Complaint*'s pale, betrayed maiden, seem explorations of the *All's Well* love relations. These connections between the play and the Sonnets do not depend on verbal echoes, but on the firmer ground of situations central to both works, and on shared tones and attitudes.

The Sonnets have been, notoriously, a hunting ground for crypto-biography. As for *All's Well*, even so conservative a critic as E. M. W. Tillyard (*Shakespeare's Problem Plays*, 1951, p. 106) thought that when he wrote the part of Bertram 'Shakespeare's personal feelings, unobjectified and untransmuted', had insinuated themselves into the writing. Such an unaltered rendering of experience is unlikely in any major author, let alone Shakespeare. Also Tillyard's phrase suggests a simpler, more monolithic Bertram than *All's Well* finally gives us. Although Tillyard's assertion is undemonstrable, it does strike a responsive note. Bertram *is* at times such a thorough wretch one is tempted to think that only personal hurt and animosity could have led the author to put him into a comedy as the 'romantic lead', so out of place is he in the role. Yet the Young Man of the Sonnets – who appears at times distasteful even through the glow of hardly earned compliment and adulation – is perfectly at home in that genre, where the Cruel Fair, whether an Adonis or a Diana, is a familiar figure.

Though there is little likelihood that in the Sonnets Shakespeare simply 'unlocked his heart', as Wordsworth put it, there is even less likelihood that the central circumstances and the attitudes worked out in the Sonnets have nothing at all to do with Shakespeare's experience or with the tone and thought of his plays, specifically of *All's Well*. In voicing the extreme anti-biographical position, scholars like W. W. Lawrence and C. J. Sisson were properly reacting against the readiness of some Victorian critics to read a *roman-à-clef* in Shakespeare's works, especially in the Sonnets. Yet ideas expressed are ideas explored; if repeated in varied contexts they can be taken to be useful to the poet in characterising experience, and so are more likely to be ideas actually held than merely brushstrokes in the definition of a character or a theatrical moment. Critical questioning of the relevance of the Sonnets has not been a wholly disinterested attempt to reassert proper rules of evidence in critical discussion. It was in part aimed at substituting for the disillusion allegedly reflected in Shakespeare's middle work more acceptable, 'wholesome' attitudes. The Problem plays, so W. W. Lawrence argued, reflected the healthy traditional attitudes of folklore and perennial morality, rather than an unpleasant scepticism.

Many of the Sonnets are addressed to the young nobleman, the unidentified Master W. H. of the dedication, a youth apparently like the elegant figure depicted in the famous Hillyard miniature of 'An Unknown Youth Leaning against a Tree among Roses'. (The initials W. H. are, by the way, discoverable in the rose-stems). The Young Man of the Sonnets is not only a social but a political type. In sonnet 106 he is a latter-day knight out of medieval chronicles, an embodiment of Elizabethan upper-class nostalgia for an earlier and presumably simpler time when noblemen had greater personal power and were less likely to be tainted by the sycophantic scramble of courtiership. The first seventeen sonnets, urging the Young Man to beget children (the question of love seems secondary) politicise their subject by linking the perpetuation of his beauty to the continuation of a noble house. The Young Man's self-withholding is the dominant theme, not only of these early sonnets, but of the powerful sonnet 94. With intense, barely controlled irony, this sonnet condemns the Young Man's unyielding self-possession and his manipulativeness. He is one of those who 'moving others, are themselves as stone'. 'Lord', 'owner', 'steward', the terms with which he is ironically described, suggest public implications in his failure to take part in the common exchange of human sympathies. Sonnet 94 also prepares for the Young Man's betrayal of the poet. The sonnet acknowledges the beauty of the Young Man's narcissistic self-sufficiency, but insists on its particular vulnerability, on the ease with which emotional isolation can succumb to corruption. The young nobleman of sonnet 94 seems in retrospect a first draft for Bertram, who is accurately prefigured also in the first lines of sonnet 96:

> Some say thy fault is youth, some wantonness,
> Some say thy grace is youth and gentle sport

and in the final lines of sonnet 94:

> The summer's flower is to the summer sweet
> Though to itself it only live and die,
> But if that flower with base infection meet,
> The basest weed outbraves his dignity:
> For sweetest things turn sourest by their deeds;
> Lilies that fester smell far worse than weeds.

Such is the Bertram of the last two acts of *All's Well*. His physical charm and presence, his apparently well-deserved military reputation, the aura of his rank (how readily the Florentines promote him and how quickly Lafew accepts him as a son-in-law!) – all these underscore the sleaziness of his attempted seduction of Diana, his thoughtless disposal of the heirloom ring, his awkward shuffling from lie to lie in the last scenes of the play. ''Tis an unseasoned courtier', says the Countess of Bertram in the first act. The seasoning he lacks is not simply the seasoning of years but a subjection to experience, which – not only to dramatists – is the experience of others, of human relationships. Bertram's affair with Diana is a relation with a face in the window and a body in the dark. Helena he knows only as a servant or a clog. With Parolles his relation is with a flattering mirror; there is nothing in it of the reciprocity of friendship. Yet these are the experiences he has chosen – experiences that demand nothing of himself.

Sonnet 121 also deals with emotional openness, specifically with sexuality, though the sonnet is concerned almost
entirely with social contexts. Its crabbed syntax and
involuted diction convey the tense quality of speech under
great emotional pressure, as in the opening lines: ''Tis
better to be vile than vile esteemed/When not to be
receives reproach of being.' The ideas are hard to speak
because they are uttered against great internal and social
resistance. After these opening lines the poem becomes
even more compressed and cryptic. Its hypothetical
argument is that it is better to actually engage in sexual
acts than only to be thought to do so when innocence
itself is inevitably judged guilty and the legitimate pleasures
of sexuality are thought vile, not because 'we' ourselves
feel them to be so, but because 'others' insist on thinking
them so. These ideas are further developed through a
series of questions that refer to the speaker's blood (i.e.
nature) as 'sportive', and to his actions (presumably sexual)
as 'frailties'. The biological, hence determinist, implications
forestall any simple moral indictment; *sportive* falls just
this side and *frailties* just the other of moral judgement.
But the critics of the poet's behaviour are unequivocally
condemned. They see him through 'false, adulterate eyes'.
They find sexuality evil 'in their wills'. The last phrase
has both the modern implications of a word like 'wilful-
ness', and Elizabethan overtones of 'will' as specifically
sexual. In the following line, 'I may be straight though
they themselves be bevel', the poet contrasts his certainty
that the censorious attitude toward sexuality is wrong, its
perceptions distorted, its conclusions an exercise of
perverse determination rather than 'natural' reason, with
his indecision or uncertainty about the morality of his
own openness. He can accept sexuality as leading to a
'just pleasure', but as he relates it to his 'sportive blood'
and to his 'frailty', he concludes nothing more than that
he *may* be straight. Despite this hesitation in judgement,
the sonnet has no hesitation about actual behaviour. Even
though it is conditional in the 'when' clause of the first

line, the choice of openness is clear. This intricately perplexing sonnet ends with yet another verbal sleight that points the question of sexuality in a political direction. The poet forbids anyone to interpret his deeds according to the 'rank thoughts' of the They of the sonnet, unless the interpreters wish to maintain a 'general evil' – namely the idea that evil is universal, that all men are bad 'and in their badness reign'.

One can argue that the awkwardly unexpected word 'reign' is a forced rhyme for 'maintain'. But the terminal sound is hardly a rare one in English, and by this time Shakespeare, though notoriously in a hurry with the endings of both his sonnets and his plays, can manage to say whatever he likes without wrenching rhymes. 'Reign' suggests that all dominant behaviour, public or private, is to be seen as an expression of depravity, depravity gloried in, royally exercised. Calling this idea a general evil is not only characterisation but critique. At the very least the word 'reign' generalises the point of view which the sonnet opposes, treating it as operating beyond the private sexual concerns with which the sonnet began.

Just who are the censorious 'They' who always have been, always will be, a menace to 'Us'? A common response is that the They of the Sonnets are Puritans and the Us of the Sonnets are our tolerant selves, roughly sharing the views of, say, Richard Hooker, whose *Laws of the Ecclesiastical Polity* is now taken to be the classic of enlightened Anglican theology of the time. Yet the differences between conservative Anglicans and Puritans were centred less on matters of civil and personal behaviour than on questions of liturgy and church government. In *All's Well*, I. iii. 90ff., Shakespeare alludes to one of these divisive questions, the reluctance of nonconformist clergy to wear the mandated cope and surplice during services. He does so in a jesting speech by Lavatch: 'Though honesty be no Puritan, yet it will do no hurt; it will wear the surplice of humility over the black gown of a big heart.' The speech is difficult; its main notion is that without being as narrow in sexual matters as the Puritans, honesty (i.e. chastity rather than celibacy) will yet not be immoral. It will, rather, like a kind of conforming nonconformist, wear the black gown typical of continental Calvinist preachers, signifying dissenting zeal, yet over the gown wear also the orthodox surplice, symbolising a willingness to compromise, to accept discipline. A passing jest – and one that probably would not have raised much of a laugh even in audiences closer than we are to Elizabethan doctrinal disputes. Yet Lavatch is, like the Fool in *Lear*, one of Shakespeare's serious clowns and attention must be paid to his matter. The passage is typical of Shakespeare's location of sexual honesty in the push-and-pull of counter-tendencies – here both surplice *and* black gown, both humility *and* big heart. Honesty belongs neither to the nonconformist nor the orthodox. Yet honesty is not a 'splitting of differences', a 'middle of the road' position. It is more like an improvisation that a gloomy or zealous view might even find self-serving and hypocritical. It recalls the hesitations and ambiguities, and above all the openness, of sonnet 121.

Historically, there was little difference between conservatives and dissenters over matters of 'practical' morality. Hooker's *Laws* had, in fact, sluggish sales, and when a popular hell-fire divine like William Perkins preached on sexual behaviour to his orthodox congregations, he would have offended very few. The 'position' of sonnet 121 is finally undoctrinal in its implied focus on the ambiguities and uncertainties of actual experience taken case by case rather than on the convenient moral categories provided by doctrine. It would be wrong to think of the They of the Sonnets as a religious faction. *They* are a transhistorical They – the public (that is the openly professed) opinion of those who have the power to define opinions as public. The detailed actualities of Elizabethan belief and behaviour are beyond the reach of sociologists and pollsters, and when belief and behaviour enter the work of even conservative Anglicans like

Sidney and Spenser they can exhibit unexpected latitudes.

If the Sonnets provide evidence of Shakespeare's thinking about sexuality and authority – admittedly evidence to be handled gingerly – they are also evidence of the social forces that shaped that thinking. The 'I' of the Sonnets is himself a kind of Helena, a provincial gaining entrée to court circles by virtue of a rare skill, forming passionate attachments 'beyond his sphere'. Like Helena he seems to have encountered a variable welcome, as the sonnets addressed to the Young Man indicate. The minutiae of class and caste are detailed with exquisite knowledge in *All's Well*. Moreover, in both Helena and the poet of the Sonnets social barriers are interiorised as moral dilemmas. For Helena her courtship of Bertram is an idolatry in thought and an ethical transgression in act; this is much of the burden of her soliloquies. The poet, who asks in sonnet 105 that his love *not* be called idolatry, is troubled not only by the fact of his status but by some of its specifically Elizabethan implications.

Sonnets 110 and 111 (the latter with a first line whose textual problems seriously affect interpretation) show us the poet arguing with his profession, giving us not only his version of the Platonic idea that acting weakens the actor's authenticity as a person, but that making himself 'a motley [clown] to the view' has 'gored' his thoughts, and that being forced to use the 'public means' of acting and writing to gain his livelihood has forced on him 'public manners'. The conjunction of blood and abstraction in the phrase 'gored thoughts' has a surreal intensity whose meaning the rest of the sonnet and the sonnet following barely explicate. What emerges, though, is familiar: earning a living exacts a set of sacrifices. First one abandons disinterestedness, then one distorts one's feelings and commitments, finally denying even brute fact. This litany of the psyche set to trade is so familiar in any period that its particular import in the Shakespearian context can easily be scanted.

If the young nobleman's emotional detachment in sonnet

94 is reprehensible, it is still closely connected with what social commentary like Castiglione's seminally important *Il Cortegiano* depicted as the courtier's highest grace: *sprezzatura*, a nonchalance in style that reflected a Renaissance idea of the psyche at liberty to reach its highest natural development. Among other things, the courtier's freedom was a freedom from self-interest, a freedom that allowed him to advise his prince properly, whatever the social and material consequences to himself. One should note in passing that for all its apparent freedom from immediate self-interest, *sprezzatura* was still the psyche set to trade, bound to sacrifice its own interests to those of the prince, who was the ultimate source of value. My colleague Nancy Lindheim has perceptively characterised the *sprezzatura* style as an 'absence of total commitment'. Such an attitude expresses a reluctance to 'become', a willingness to 'be', in effect a satisfaction with things as they are. This is obviously the expression of a dominant, rather than of an aspiring class. Prince Hal exhibited the cool self-respecting style of *sprezzatura* when, despite the provocation and his own stake in the matter, he allowed Falstaff to claim the triumph over the rebel Hotspur as his own, rather than squabble over honours due.

The worst, in the Renaissance proverb, was a corruption of the best. The total emotional disengagement of the Young Man is a corrupt version of the courtier's freedom from self-serving attachments. It is this proximity of the best and the worst that makes for difficult judgements of the aristocratic style and for the deceptive first appearances of certain characters. What seems odd to us in Helena's choice may be due in part to her confusion of distance with merit, and her 'ambition', too, may be the admiration of an ideal rather than simple status-seeking. Helena's view of Bertram as if from a sphere below emphasises, as do 'His arched brows, his hawking eye, his curls', those aspects of appearance which translate in the theatre to the commanding, the well-cared-for look that defines aristocratic presence.

Wholly opposite to such a lofty poise and psychological self-sufficiency, with their promise to conventional Elizabethan thought of unwarped perception and disinterested insight, was the actual condition of the actor-dramatist, a 'motley' singing for his supper, a mere performer. The social cachet of theatrical people today – now a citizen royalty – simply did not exist. They were at best hobbies of royal households or the minor ornaments of upper aristocratic occasions, although their value in propaganda, in acting out the social fictions of status, and their other ancillary uses to the State were increasingly recognised. It was only noble sponsorship and patronage, which carried the permission to style themselves servants – i.e. The Lord Chamberlain's Men, the King's Men (Shakespeare's companies) – that kept the acting troupes from being 'adjudged and deemed rogues, vagabonds, and sturdy beggars', and punished as such according to the Act of 1597. The Act was directed, it is true, primarily against 'masterless men' of whom the London Council thought there were far too many. But the patronage of the nobility frustrated attempts by City authorities to control the players, and this token attempt at regulation was as far as they could go. The Act nevertheless indicates the social status of the profession and the attitude toward it held firmly by most City officials and seconded by shopkeepers and others who considered the theatre a nuisance at best, at worst an enemy to religion and public order and an attractive opportunity for the working apprentice to waste time and money. For all the differences in social structure, however, the theatre, as today, bridged 'the mightiest space in fortune', bringing together men and women of diverse social levels – a William Shakespeare, writer-player, with a Master W. H. and (unless the two are one) a third Earl of Southampton.

By some accounts the third Earl, Henry Wriothesley, was as handsome as he was accomplished. Through most of his minority he had been the royal ward of Lord Burleigh, the Lord Treasurer. Southampton, smiled on

by the Queen and an intimate of Essex, was a patron of
scholars and poets and, according to Thomas Nashe's
dedication to him of a work of prose fiction, *The
Unfortunate Traveller*, 'a dear lover and cherisher . . . as
well of the lovers of poets, as of poets themselves'. Given
the restrictions of the age, the theatre gave Shakespeare
an unusual opportunity to observe at first hand the usually
distant top of Elizabethan society. Yet one must add that
the 'friendship' and the 'love' of the Sonnets seem always
to be clouded by formality, a brittle remoteness that goes
beyond the strained proprieties such relationships rarely
avoid in any period.

It is too easy to cast Southampton as the original of
Bertram, though the two were wards and Southampton
was also a conscientious objector to matrimony, having
resisted with some vacillation Burleigh's attempts to
marry the young man off to his granddaughter. Yet after
one sets aside the notion of portraiture, there remains the
common-sense conclusion that acquaintance, speculation
and report of the likes of such figures as Southampton
entered into the making of the Sonnets and plays such as
All's Well. The alternative is less believable.

The contrasts in social status and outlook between the
poet and the Young Man of the Sonnets are stated with
a mixture of regret and irony in sonnet 87, beginning
with the autumnal line:

> Farewell, thou art too dear for my possessing,

and ending with the remarkable couplet:

> Thus have I had thee, as a dream doth flatter,
> In sleep a king, but waking no such matter.

The couplet suggests the impression of illusion and
inauthenticity felt by the poet as he considers his
'friendship' with the Young Man. This illusory quality is
defined in the sonnet as a psychological difference which
flows from the disparity of status; 'how do I hold thee
but by thy granting?' the poet asks. For all the poet's

love, his psychologically and socially necessary self-effacement must keep the relation from being reciprocal; it is ever dependent on permission, hence fragile and unreal. The final couplet underscores this fragility of feeling at being made royal, ennobled through illusion – again the emotions are mediated by status. There is a parallel between the poet's fragile relation with the Young Man and the actual fragility of his own status as actor-playwright, hence doubly the creator of fictive nobility. If we are to believe the legend that Shakespeare acted the role of the Ghost in *Hamlet* he could say that he had been indeed 'In sleep a king, but waking no such matter'. The consciousness of having played or created roles to which he was subjected probably strengthened the already emerging dream-triad of love, art and life in Shakespeare's work.

The poet may protest in sonnet 91 that 'Thy love is better than high birth to me/Richer than wealth . . .', yet the absence of narrow self-interest on his part does not eliminate differences in status as root causes of both attraction and estrangement. The Young Man's glittering remoteness and the poet's self-effacement are unavoidable indices of those differences. More importantly, though the poet may protest at the subjugation to Fortune that, in fact, drives him to poetry, his commitment to poetry is profound, and thus at odds with the *sprezzatura* style's 'absence of total commitment'.

In his *Apology for Poetry*, Sir Philip Sidney was at some pains to deflect the reader's attention from the social anomaly of a gentleman of high rank (as Sidney was) expending so much learning and effort on a subject usually the concern of clerks and ambitious minor office-holders. Poetry may have been a help to preferment in Elizabethan times, but the standard view of it from above is best summarised in Bacon's epithet 'toys' for theatrical entertainments – or, so the story goes – Burleigh's irritable attempt to deny Edmund Spenser a grant of £50 for *The Faerie Queene*: 'All that for a song?' Sidney's *Apology* begins with an amusing and mildly self-deprecatory anecdote about his days as a student of the aristocratic art of horsemanship, and ends with the joking wish that detractors of poetry may fail in the courtship of ladies for want of the ability to write a decent sonnet. Bracketed by these lightly apologetic evidences of upper-class cachet is a total commitment to art.

Part of the rhetorical task of the Sonnets is similar: how to manage a conformity to the biases of the aristocratic outlook without abandoning the total commitment to art. If the sonnets on the poet's theatrical career show the inevitable failure of the task, sonnet 39 is even more inclusive. The poet asks: 'O how thy worth with manners may I sing?' The issue is one of protocol, here not *mere* protocol, but the compatibility of celebrating value in general and beauty in particular, that is of writing poetry at all within the aristocratic code. In writing poetry rather than drama there is no obvious goring of thoughts or pandering to 'public manners'. But sonnet 39 presents more intimately and profoundly the same dilemma regarding poetry that is presented in the sonnets on theatre. If, in fact, friendship is 'one soul in bodies twain', then how can the poetry of its celebration be anything but self-interested and self-aggrandising? The issue is turned into a pretty paradox at several points. The sonnet ends with a proposal that sounds ominous despite the filigree elegance of its development from the self-interested nature of praise voiced in the fourth line: 'Even for this, let us divided live.'

Through the elegance and intricacy of the idea, the resolution of the dilemma is clear enough. The poet's allegiances are to the poem, hence to a recognition of the necessary social distance imposed not only by the fact of his inferior status or the nature of the theatre, but by his own commitment to poetry. Even when the 'gap in fortune' may be bridged by the Young Man's indulgent recognition of the superior compliment of a poem or of the love that caused it, the connection is momentary and fragile, always shadowed by a recognition of the alien commitments to poetry on which it depends.

The commitment to poetry, however, is not only a commitment to art, but to an openness and mutuality of feeling that the estrangements of status and the uncommitted style do not permit. The painful, obsessive quality of the poet's love for the Young Man and its self-effacement are in the 'poetic', hardly in the 'noble' style. Finally, the poet's choice is for the problematic openness of sonnet 121 over the lordly closed-heartedness of sonnet 94. With the most untypical of princes, Hamlet, the poet chooses to unpack his heart with words, like a male whore, a 'stallion'. Lower on the 'noble' scale one cannot go, yet the poet evidently accepts the implications of committing himself to such a career.

The twin themes of status and sexuality are taken several stages further in the sonnets to the Dark Lady. She represents the new age as the Young Man represented the old. Where the Young Man withheld feeling, the Dark Lady offered it – intensely but problematically. The poet had exchanged for his 'master-mistress' a mistress who was a master of pragmatic artifice. These sonnets have been condemned as cynical, their tone and matter attributed to a supposed emotional crisis during which Shakespeare also wrote the so-called Dark Comedies – notably *All's Well* and *Measure for Measure*. In common usage the epithet 'cynicism' is a relative term, depending more on how the user distributes 'is' and 'ought' over the topography of experience than on any care for the philosophic meaning of the term. The central sonnet in the Dark Lady cluster, sonnet 138, states its theme in the first two lines:

> When my love swears that she is made of truth
> I do believe her though I know she lies

and explicates its puns and outlook in the final couplet:

> Therefore I lie with her, and she with me,
> And in our faults by lies we flattered be.

Is this cynicism, or only the rueful acceptance of 'half a loaf?' To say that 'half a loaf is better than none' is to acknowledge the necessity of bread. Like the ending of *All's Well*, sonnet 138 plaits together satisfaction and failure, the pleasures of deceiving and being deceived, and the pains of being undeceived. None of the play's characters voices the total understanding of the poet or precisely his – that is, the play's – tone of rueful acceptance. Yet after her assignation with Bertram, Helena comes fairly close. And the ending of *All's Well* affects some readers as does the end of sonnet 138.

This double-edged outlook of sonnet 138, like the relation it treats, accepts and even amusingly enjoys (see also sonnets, 130, 135) a love that both countenances and depends on infidelity and untruth. The sonnet can be understood in the psychological contexts it provides, but also, as can the play, in the grimmer context offered by the famous sonnet 129 on lust. Most of the sonnet's condemnations of lust were proverbial, as were the few statements insisting on what the poem itself warrants our calling the attractiveness of lust:

Before, a joy proposed, behind, a dream.
All this the world well knows, yet none knows well
To shun the heaven that leads men to this hell.

What was perhaps a novelty was the letter and spirit of the last three lines. These concluding lines make it difficult to reduce the equivocal word 'dream' to '*empty* dream' or to moralise away the paradox – a hell *yet* a heaven – spoken of physical sexuality unattached to ceremony, law or civility. No question the sonnet is finally condemnatory. Even when the lust is Bertram's and it results only in his bedding his own wife, it is 'yet a sinful fact', as Helena says. But this does not prevent Helena from also observing:

O strange men!
That can such sweet use make of what they hate
When saucy trusting of the cozened thoughts

38 *All's Well That Ends Well*

> Defiles the pitchy night; so lust doth play
> With what it loathes . . .
>
> (IV. iv. 21–4)

Helena's language has the sonnet triad of condemnation ('cozened', 'defiles'), magnetic sensuality ('sweet', 'play') and wondering recognition of their partnership ('strange', 'sweet'–'hate', 'play'–'loathes'). It is useful to recognise the difference between merely dismissive moralities, positions alert to but rejecting 'temptations', and the view of the couplet and hence of the sonnet, condemning the extremes to which lust can lead ('murderous', 'bloody', 'savage'), yet recognising the emotional and moral ambiguities that follow from the impossibility of uprooting it. If lust is indeed a human 'given', an ineradicable tendency, then perhaps the perceptions that lead to Calvinism can with equal logic lead to something quite different, the problematic view of sexual behaviour given us in sonnet 129.

Elsewhere, however, sonnet 129 seems to suggest something even more exculpating than human weakness in the face of lust. Lust is 'as a swallowed bait/On purpose laid to make the taker mad'. One can argue that the 'as' makes the idea of entrapment merely metaphoric. Yet the sonnet seems to allow the unshunnable 'heaven' of the couplet to tell against both the dismissive and optimistically cautionary attitudes. Is it an accident that of the eight proverbial antecedents of the sonnet given by Stephen Booth (p. 441) five concern love, one 'extremes' and two 'pleasures'? A significant antecedent is 'Love's beginning is fear, middle sin, end grief and annoyance', which, if we ignore its narrative sequence, suggests the proverbial quality of the affective spectrum of the Sonnets. To return to the Dark Lady sonnets in the context provided by 121 and 129 is to understand the poet's acceptance of the half-loaf of physical obsession as both a rueful and a willing acceptance of actuality: the love-relationship as one in which idealities are unlikely and physical needs beyond complete control.

Moralist, libertine, paradox-monger; social victim, sycophant, parvenu: the difficulty with such summary notions is that character and idea in neither *All's Well* nor the Sonnets fit such small neat shapes. Northrop Frye once remarked that Shakespeare gave each play just the ideas it seems to need. Like props and characters ideas earn their literary keep not through any intrinsic merit but through a demand for them in the total work. Yet neither the Sonnets nor the plays show Shakespeare as the chameleon poet, only 'myriad-minded', to use Coleridge's phrase. The multiplicity and conditionality have a bias towards openness and relativity of judgement. Most of Shakespeare's comedies end with some reminder of a human flaw and a demurrer from happiness. Antonio, the beneficent *Merchant of Venice*, is unpartnered (forever?) as the play ends. Malvolio shakes his fist at the *Twelfth Night* weddings. *Love's Labour's Lost* does not 'end like an old play'. Jacks will not have their Jills till a year's mourning (and penance) are over. The moral shapes of theatrical genres are evidently too absolute, too neat for an observer of the actual, and the realities that lie just beyond every fifth act call into question the premises on which it ends. Shakespeare is fond of having the shadow of those realities visible at the wedding feasts. It is hardly a great risk since all along the audience has known it was in the theatre. Indeed Shakespeare's demurrers are not only an expression of conviction but a compliment to his patrons' intelligence. In *All's Well*, however, the risk is great indeed, approaching the intellectual daring of the Sonnets.

· 3 ·

Power and Status

The order of the Sonnets, like much else about them, promises to remain a subject of controversy, but as they stand the Sonnets exhibit a progressive departure from the orthodox attitudes concerning sexuality and power of the initial poems, an increasingly psychological self-representation and self-division in the sonnet-poet, and an increasing daring in their exploration of his social and moral situation. One could hardly expect that the author of these Sonnets, whose intermittent and cloudy narrative threw a proportionately greater emphasis on their themes and emotions, would have left power, status and sexuality as he found them in Boccaccio, where they are employed only as obstacle or motive for Giletta's triumph. Because of the brevity of his tale and its perspective, the single-minded concern with Giletta's story, Boccaccio barely sketches the social ambience in which it takes place. By contrast *All's Well* is as much a play about power and status as it is about love. The social organisation of a noble estate and a royal court are drawn in detail. The characters' self-presentation and modes of address exhibit fine gradations of status, placing Shakespeare in the line of English-watchers that runs through Jane Austen, Trollope and Thackeray. Considerations of caste and status shape the thought and behaviour of the play's leading figures, and the implications of social issues suggest

directions for the audience's response. The play's social
vision is not merely determinist, however. Characters can
respond to one another as superiors, equals or as 'creatures
of another place' [status], and the social harmony that
ends the comedy is glaringly at odds with the incongruity
of the principals. The 'new family' created by marriage
is, for once in Shakespeare, *not* symbolic of a larger social
order to which fifth-act weddings in comedies usually
point.

If this seems a mischievous way of dealing with the
traditional idea of comedy, and romantic comedy in
particular, it is matched by the way Shakespeare represents
– and questions – power and status. The King of France
does have absolute power over his courtiers, the Countess
of Rossillion over her household, and Bertram over his
Florentine troops. Everyone in the play gains status from
an association with a court, a household, or an institution,
and – the King excepted – must defer to someone with
higher status, inherent or assimilated. Yet this gridwork
of power, status and deference proves to be a fragile
cobweb in *All's Well*. Not only 'Sceptre and crown/Must
tumble down' at the push of disease and death, but
prerogative and station are self-exposed by their rhetoric,
mocked by the witty, overturned by the bold and gifted
and finally made somewhat irrelevant by the weak and
decent. The fifth act of *All's Well* shows everyone fumbling
but Helena and her allies, though theirs may well seem a
worthless success. Yet such success as it is has been
brought about by a natural, heartfelt alliance of the
deprived. A widow of high station powerless to keep her
young son at home befriends a young woman of low
station who is aided rather inconclusively by a King, but
decisively by another widow whose main concern is her
own daughter. The play questions the conventions of
power and status not only through intellectual argument
and turns of plot, but through parallel lines of construction
that give nominal power to the warrior males but effective
power to an alliance of women – all of them lacking, if

not always wanting, husbands, fathers or lovers.

Boccaccio is unclear about the circumstances under which Beltramo is sent to Paris. We learn only that 'when his father was deade, [he] left under the royall custody of the King'. Nothing is said of Beltramo's mother, so that royal custody may be interpreted as a gracious act of protective sympathy extended to a noble orphan. By inventing a Countess of Rossillion, a mother for Bertram, Shakespeare clarifies at once (for Elizabethan audiences at least) the precise circumstances of Bertram's departure. Bertram's own words present his situation: 'I must attend his majesty's command, to whom I am now in ward, evermore in subjection.' The Countess's first speech, in which she compares the 'delivering' of Bertram to burying a second husband, has been taken as a grim pun on childbirth ('the delivery of a son into the world of responsibility'), an Oedipal motif, and as a first sounding of a funereal, 'death-haunted quality' in the play. But Bertram's last phrase is more relevant and less metaphoric. The Countess is literally delivering, turning over, her son to Lafew as the King's agent, something she is required to do by law, and the death of her husband is precisely the occasion of this second loss. Under feudal law the King controlled the estates of any of his tenants-in-chief who were unlucky enough to inherit them before reaching the age of twenty-one. Further, the King could dispose of such wards in marriage at his will. Both 'rights' are related to the historical origins of land-tenure in exchange for military service. The Crown presumably guaranteed the continuity of such service through its wardship and marriage rights.

In 1540 the Tudors instituted a Court of Wards, thus enabling the Crown to better control and, if it wished, to sell its rights over the persons of its wards and over their estates. The Court was established to strengthen government finances during the later years of Henry VIII's reign, and specifically to take advantage of the increases in feudal dues attending the dissolution of the monasteries and the marketing of monastic lands. In practice, the selling of wards was successful in consolidating royal social control and in raising revenues not only for the Crown but for the guardian-purchasers of wards. Guardians came from a wide social range; Burleigh and Leicester were guardians of wards as were Ambrose Jenny, the Queen's footman, and Dr Smith, her physician. Peers could buy wealthy wards, grasp quick profits, and then marry their wards or marry them off to their children. In defence of their young, prudent parents could follow the example of the dying Earl of Dorset. The Earl hastily married off his son Richard in order to frustrate the Duke of Lennox, who was waiting impatiently for the Earl's death-knell so he could purchase the heir. What had been consolidated into a going concern under Henry VIII became a roaring success under Elizabeth. The income of the Court of Wards rose 48 per cent during the last three years of Elizabeth's reign.

Under Elizabeth the peerage itself seems to have been for the most part protected from the worst abuses of the system, although sons and daughters of peers were still married off according to the advantage of their guardians, rather than according to their own best interests. Wards did have a nominal legal protection against what was called 'disparagement', the imposition of gross misalliances of rank, and they could, at great cost, buy their way out of unwanted marriages. But this was lean comfort, no comfort at all if the wards were very young and could barely appreciate, let alone protest, their fate.

The historian Joel Hurstfield writes that 'of lawsuits for disparagement I have been able to trace no evidence whatsoever'. Of 'direct action to prevent disparagement', he writes that 'we have a little evidence, including Shakespeare's Bertram who, as a nobleman, refused on the ground of disparagement the proffered marriage to a poor physician's daughter'.

The sometimes violent results of such arranged marriages were depicted in several plays: *A Yorkshire Tragedy*, written very shortly after *All's Well* and once attributed to Shakespeare, and George Wilkins' *The Miseries of Inforst Marriage* (1607). It is odd to consider Bertram as a luckless casualty of social injustice, an immediate forerunner of the sympathetic protagonists of popular stage plays, and hence a small icon of the struggle for civil freedom. Yet even had he not been the King's ward, a Bertram, like Hamlet, would not have 'carved for himself'. While *A Yorkshire Tragedy* and Wilkins' *Miseries* and Marston's *Scourge of Villainy* decried the injustices of wardship and imposed marriage, and everyone from James I down seemed to agree, the dominant role of parents and guardians in matchmaking during the late sixteenth and early seventeenth centuries typically decreased only as one descended the social ladder. Bertram was heir to great lands and power. Rossillion was 'an old province of France', the dead Count a mate-in-arms of the King, the young Count deferred to by his fellow officers and by the Florentines, who immediately made him 'the general of our horse'. Shakespeare emphasises the point. Boccaccio's Beltramo is made only 'captaine of a certaine number of men, continuing in their [the Florentines'] service a long time', presumably without further advancement. Such a figure as Bertram could hardly be allowed to contract a marriage with *anybody*.

The Elizabethan realities of marriage among the highborn could be closer to the fairy-tale arbitrariness of royal intervention than was comfortable. Such marriages were political, economic, and in some cases even military alliances, and Elizabeth joined jealousy with prudence when she took offence at her courtiers' attempts to contract marriages without her knowledge and approval. Sir Francis Walsingham, an influential member of the Privy Council and its Principal Secretary, might have disingenuously thought himself 'no person of that state but that it may be thought a presumption for me to trouble her Majesty with a private matter between a free gentleman [Philip Sidney] of equal calling with my daughter [Frances]', but the Queen thought otherwise. She had an instant negative reaction to this alliance between Protestant activitists. But Elizabeth dealt less harshly with Sidney than she had dealt or was to deal with other transgressors. After a few weeks she allowed herself to be won over to the marriage, exacting only a further delay as punishment for the indiscretion of the matchmakers. Elizabeth's reservations about Sidney's marriage were typical of the wariness with which she regarded all her courtiers' courtships. After his forced 'retirement' from court for his role in opposing the intended marriage of the Queen to Alençon, Sidney made his peace with Elizabeth by offering her a symbolic gift – a jewel-encrusted whip.

The point of all this is that *All's Well* opens with a social thunderclap which has been muffled by the passage of social history. It is doubtful that historical reconstruction alone will enable a modern audience to feel at once, though it may help us to 'appreciate', the intensity that hovers about the speeches at the very beginning of the first scene of *All's Well*, a moment in any case subject to neglect because of the audience's yet unfocused attention. The Countess is losing her son, not because in the ordinary course of the life of a peer he must go off to the kind of civil finishing school constituted by court attendance, but because his father has died. What adds to her grief at the loss of her husband is that the Countess is being treated as a non-mother, for purposes of law an un-person, and her son – foolish as she knows him to be – made a kind of artificial orphan. When she says that her son is an 'unseasoned' courtier, the Countess is concerned with Bertram's particular limitations, but she is also stating that he is simply not ready to leave the nest. This accounts for the gracious warmth of Lafew's reassurances. It accounts, too, for the very presence of Lafew, an old comrade of the King's, as the King's agent. Sending him is a royal compliment also intended as reassurance to the Countess.

The seriousness of the occasion – which Elizabethan audiences would have grasped as modern audiences do not – somewhat mitigates the petulance of Bertram's first speech. Bertram, too, in going mourns again his father's death because of its effect on his future: if only the old man had lived until Bertram was twenty-one! (Like Helena he overlays mourning with a more selfish reflexive grief.) The old Count of Rossillion should have died hereafter, when Bertram was twenty-one and could have inherited, and had the management of himself and his estates. Now Bertram 'must attend his majesty's command', to whom he is 'now in ward, evermore in subjection'. The rhythm of the clause, three almost equally long units, parallel in the speaking and hence cumulatively emphatic, each unit ending on a significant word, 'command', 'ward', 'subjection', conveys its heavy tone. What an actor does with the phrase 'evermore in subjection' will depend on his sense of Bertram's virtual age. A Bertram of twenty saying 'evermore' is petulant; a Bertram of seventeen, with four years of fending off authority ahead of him, might be excused the phrase.

What sort of treatment lies ahead of Bertram as ward is evidenced almost at once. 'What is it, my good lord, the King languishes of?' Bertram asks Lafew, taking care that the honorific term of address is extended by the deferential 'my good' and emphasised by its interruption of the typical flow of syntax. Lafew answers considerately but laconically and with the minimal term of politeness. 'A fistula, my lord.' But Bertram persists in this line of questioning, which has rather inconsiderately interrupted the exchange between Lafew and the Countess concerning Helena's late father, the great physician Gerard de Narbon. Not only has young Bertram breached etiquette, but he has intruded on a subject of particular import to old people – health. When Bertram goes on with this breach, commenting on the King's fistula that 'I heard not of it before', he gets a smart flick of the lash. Turning briefly to him, Lafew responds with 'I would it were not notorious', which is as much as to say, 'You, young man, are one of the outsiders I hoped would not be gossiping about the King's intimate affairs'. And then without pause, addressing the Countess, Lafew compounds the slight by actually noticing the lowly Helena. Bertram is triply rebuked. This seems to promise that at the Court his interruptions will get no motherly indulgence; his concern that as a figure of importance he be kept *au courant* will be treated as presumption, and he will discover that a mere doctor's daughter can be at least as much an object of polite interest as the ward-heir to Rossillion. After the Countess has satisfied Lafew's question and the audience's about Helena, Bertram speaks again, in what may be taken as a further interruption. Lafew again turns on him: 'How understand we that?' The Countess prevents a reply by granting Bertram her blessing, but in a form that initially is also a half-implied rebuke, bidding Bertram succeed his father in manners as he does in appearance. The Countess hopes for her son precisely that character she has just attributed to Helena, but where her description of Helena is hopeful, her wish for Bertram is stated in terms of a struggle unresolved. She follows her blessing with a few practical rules that seem irrelevant in view of the larger unresolved problems she sees in Bertram's character, and the passage ends with a gloomy plea to Lafew: 'good my lord/Advise him.' Lafew's answer, hardly reassuring, is a cryptic prediction that the Count Bertram will get the best he deserves.

Bertram's exit speech, a rather condescending instruction to Helena to be 'comfortable' to his mother, underlines his insistence on her inferior rank in the unnecessary reminder that the Countess is 'your mistress'. The tirelessly alert Lafew makes Bertram's snobbery unmistakable by immediately and graciously addressing Helena: 'Farewell, pretty lady; you must hold the credit of your father.' Both Lafew's epithet and his redefinition of Helena's task as not that of a servant, but an inheritor, and one who must hold, that is continue rather than, as Bertram must,

achieve a reputation, are subtle compliments. In this first
part of the scene Bertram does not escape Lafew's scrutiny
for a moment. His wardship has indeed begun, and we
now learn that 'evermore in subjection' can also mean
subjection every moment. The BBC *All's Well* showed
Bertram at the Court in Act 2 carrying a large flask evidently
filled with the King's urine. The image is a striking visual
correlative of Bertram's status as royal ward.

The most telling exercise of the King's power is, of
course, his enforcing of Bertram's marriage to Helena.
Helena's preparation for her choice is carefully presented.
In Painter the King promises Giletta a husband 'of right
good worship and estimation', which accurately renders
Boccaccio's equally modest and general phrase *'bene e
altamente'*. As she negotiates her reward for curing the
King, the terms she employs indicate that Shakespeare is
precisely aware of the King's powers over his wards.
Helena will request as husband only 'such a one, thy
vassal, whom I know/Is free for me to ask, thee to
bestow'. She is careful to eliminate from her choice any
of the King's children or 'other of your blood'. Here
Shakespeare follows both Painter and Boccaccio. That he
can follow his fourteenth-century original so closely on
this point and be clearly understood in early seventeenth-
century terms is due to a historical anomaly: the long
persistence of medieval land-tenure in England. Hence the
importance of Helena's use of the triggering phrase, 'thy
vassal'. As a tenant-in-chief, Bertram inherits Rossillion
in exchange for military service, hence his wardship and
his vulnerability to the King's wishes. Helena's, and
Giletta's, exclusion of members of the royal house from
her choice is a reasonable precaution against 'disparagement'. But is the King free to bestow *any* of his wards
on Helena without risking the objection of misalliance?
To pursue the question is not to forget that these are
fictive creatures but to consider Shakespeare's imaginative
alteration of Boccaccio's materials.

Giletta was rich, an heiress, something of a 'catch' if

we are to believe the solicitude of her kinsfolk, her many
suitors and the description of her setting off on pilgrimage
'well furnished with silver and precious Jewels, with her
maide, and one of her kinsemen'. Giletta may content
'her selfe, with the state of a poor pilgrime', but this is a
matter of policy. Helena, however, is heiress only to a
set of medical prescriptions. Her 'friends' (i.e. relatives)
'were poor, but honest', as she protests to the Countess.
When she sets off to Paris she requires, and receives,
'Means and attendants' from the Countess, on whom
she is completely dependent. Helena proclaims herself
'wealthiest' in her modest chastity. Bertram's phrase 'A
poor physician's daughter' is echoed by the King, who
determines to add honour and wealth to the virtue that
is Helena's dowry. In short Shakespeare is at great pains
to alter his source in this detail of Helena's wealth – with
all its implications for social status – while keeping much
else as it is in Boccaccio.

To reinvent the heiress Giletta as a poor physician's
Helena was to alter what was marginally conceivable as a
marriage in early seventeenth-century England to what
was imaginable only in fiction; to alter a social curiosity
into something close to a fairy-tale. Around 1604 the
terms 'poor physician' and 'poor physician's daughter'
would have been almost as much an oxymoron as today.
The standard physician's fee was one angel, a gold coin
equivalent to ten shillings, and visits were made more
frequently then than now. The standard lawyer's fee was
ten groats for a consultation. The weekly wage for artisans
and schoolmasters was about six shillings; one penny was
the minimum price of admission to a public theatre.
Shakespeare's son-in-law, who styled himself a 'gentleman', was himself the son of a well-to-do physician.
Despite having neither a Royal College of Physicians
licence nor a Bishop's licence he developed a lucrative and
in part aristocratic practice after moving to Stratford
around 1600. His clinical notes were thought sufficiently
valuable to be translated from the Latin and issued

posthumously as *Observations on English Bodies*. In 1626 he paid a fine of £12 rather than accept the knighthood then imposed on men of wealth, but his daughter Elizabeth, Shakespeare's granddaughter, was to take a second husband, Bernard (or Barnard), later knighted by Charles II for loyalty during the Interregnum.

Physicians, especially those licensed by the College of Physicians, were generally well-off, moved easily among gentry and nobility and had then as now considerable social and economic power. In 1603, James I knighted his physician, Sir William Paddy; he also knighted an important physician, Sir Theodore Touquet de Mayerne, who was Baron d'Aubonne in his own right. Just how powerful the College of Physicians could be is evidenced by their having taken on Sir Francis Walsingham on three occasions in an effort to maintain their control over medical practice. In each case the College won, though among their targets were a herbalist, Margaret Kenwix, who had impressed the Queen, and Walsingham's own doctor, the intriguingly named Mr Not. After his last defeat Walsingham offered the College his apologies and agreed never again to act in any matter opposed to their benefit and dignity.

The intense interest in medicine of some of the nobility, especially of aristocratic women, should hardly seem eccentric. For charitable and merely prudential reasons it was useful to know how to minister to one's tenants, servants, dependants, even one's self in cases of emergency – especially in Elizabethan conditions of slow communication and thinly-spread professional advice. My colleague David Hoeniger, in a work now being published, cites a long list of noble medical adepts of the period, including Francis Bacon's mother, who was the daughter of Sir Anthony Coke; the wife of the powerful Lord Burleigh; Lady Anthony Mildmay; the Countess of Arundel and others. Lady Margaret Hoby's diary (1599–1605) 'tells us how, mainly in the country, she performed all sorts of medical activities, including some daring surgery'. Indeed, 'she became an army surgeon in the time of James I, and she was not the only one'. Helena had a good number of noble predecessors.

None of this, however, places the medical profession or its families in Bertram's rarified sphere of the nobility. Yet the university education of most physicians and the critical nature of their profession did make for easy social relations and common bonds with their social superiors. The intermarriage of the inheritors of landed estates and the daughters of men with financial, commercial or professional interests is difficult to estimate. Table 7.8, on p. 248 of L. and J. Stone's *An Open Elite? England 1540–1880* (1984) suggests something between five and eight per cent as a reasonable guess at the extent of such intermarriages in the first decade of the seventeenth century – hardly common, though there were more than enough to have been talked about. Most of the alliances between landed and professional families would have involved the daughters of lawyers and office-holders. There is no indication of the number of upwardly mobile medical heiresses, though in all likelihood there were very few. In the nature of things, managing *English Bodies* is less elegant and acceptable socially than managing English property. In seventeenth-century terms, then, an English Beltramo–Giletta alliance might have been represented as rare and most uncomfortable but not quite to *all* observers as a dreadful instance of disparagement. But to make Helena poor and lowly, a servant in the household, as she is not in Boccaccio, is to put the marriage far out of reach.

How determined Shakespeare was on this change of status should be clear from the strain on audience credulity it involved. Like Gerard de Narbon, Shakespeare's son-in-law was a 'country doctor', similarly famous in his profession, known and valued if not by the King of France then by the Earl of Warwick. On his death, his daughter Elizabeth, Shakespeare's granddaughter, had prospects that were like those of Giletta, and she was indeed ultimately married to a landed knight in easy circumstances. Helena could have no such prospects.

Successive historical audiences bring with them a different knowledge and sensibility which affect their reception of the plays they see. In dealing with his own time, the only one he deeply knows or can care deeply about, the writer neutralises some of its peculiar qualities and takes advantage of others: alluding to or sharing the topical and the historical biases, mocking the fashionable, pushing with and against ephemeral but concrete actuality. However far afield it goes, the imagination, especially the theatrical imagination, begins with what is literally so. In taking his risk with the reinvention of rich Giletta as poor Helena, Shakespeare prepared the way for a number of complex remotivations of Boccaccio's characters and for some related excursions into ideology that had no precedent in the *Decameron*. As Shakespeare has remade the story of *All's Well*, the Bertram–Helena match is clearly an instance of disparagement. Boccaccio's King cajoles and orders; Shakespeare's King must provide a lecture on moral sociology that would not have been out of place in England at any time from the mid-sixteenth century until the Second World War, one of those universally gratifying expressions of self-justification that deference societies regularly provide. For the moment it is enough to recall that the King's lecture on virtue and status is meant to rationalise a completely arbitrary and legally questionable act.

Less conventional is the motivation of Shakespeare's best invention, the Countess of Rossillion. The Countess's partiality to Helena is intensified because Bertram is being taken from her and because the contrast between the two children is so extreme. When in Act 1 Scene 3 the Steward offers to relate what he has overheard of Helena's secret thoughts, evidently the Countess bridles since the Steward's second speech is defensive and her response is an irritated questioning of the propriety of Lavatch's presence at the proposed revelations. When her comical palaver with Lavatch is over and she dispatches him to fetch Helena, the Countess employs a revealing locution: 'Sirrah, tell my gentlewoman I would speak with her – Helen I mean.' No doubt the Countess of Rossillion had several gentlewomen. Although they may add bustle to the modern stage, they do not reach the *dramatis personae* of *All's Well*. There was thus no need to specify Helena in the command to Lavatch. The term 'gentlewoman' is primarily a term of assimilated status, not to be taken literally as proof of membership in the gentry. The Second Gravedigger in *Hamlet* can use the term 'gentlewoman' of the dead Ophelia in making his case that the high-born have privileges even after death, but generally the term is used as a compliment to the gentlewoman's mistress, from whom some small warmth of deference falls on the servant. The Countess's feeling for Helena does not fit this brittle mould. She does not think of Helena as merely filling any, let alone a servant's, household role, but as herself – Helen. The omission of the final syllable makes the name less formal and posh and associates it with what follows immediately, Lavatch's rhyme on Helen of Troy. The Steward, too, speaks of her as Helen, using the informal 'Helen' as condescension. In the movingly intimate scene which follows later, Helena slowly and painfully reveals her love under the kind promptings of the Countess, who addresses her by name four times, all of them as Helen.

If the Countess refuses to insist on Helena's class role, she also refuses to insist on her own, rejecting Helena's term of address, 'Mine honourable mistress', in the response, 'Nay, a mother'. Shakespeare makes sure that Helena's subsequent confession of love for Bertram is entwined with questions of social status. Helena retreats from accepting the tender fiction of a mother–daughter relation with the Countess lest it dwindle her love for Bertram to the merely sisterly. In doing so, however, she argues:

The Count Rossillion cannot be my brother.
I am from humble, he from honoured name;

No note upon my parents, his all noble.
My master, my dear lord he is; and I
His servant live, and will his vassal die.

The speech has several functions. After this there can
be no doubt that Shakespeare is preparing for the issue
of disparagement. Nor can the Countess doubt that what
she has heard and suspected is indeed true. But she *can*
doubt that Helena will remain content with her current
state. In theatrical speech, revelation is often also conceal-
ment. Only a few lines later the Countess proposes the
role that will allow Helena to be her daughter yet remain
no sister to Bertram: 'my daughter-in-law'. She follows
this immediately with the heartfelt prayer: 'God shield
you mean it not!'

The Countess of Rossillion is neither an eccentric nor
an egalitarian. She accepts with a resigned good grace not
only the forced departure of her son but the royal efforts
to make the blow more palatable. Everything in her speech
and in the management of her servants shows her to be
wholly at ease in her role of chatelaine. Her slightly
shocked and apprehensive response to Helena's confession
of love has to be balanced against the loving kindness
with which she earlier guessed Helena's emotional situation
and saw it also as once her own. The remainder of the
scene between them is one of the most movingly intimate
Shakespeare ever wrote for women – for boy actors, or
for a boy and an almost adult male actor, one should say.
It is all tingling intimation, for what it conveys is the
development of an unspoken and vague alliance to see
beyond a great social barrier; unspoken not only because
it is yet only partly formed and floating on a nameless
hope, but unspoken because both women are deeply
conscious of how at odds with their natures (or nurtures,
at least) is Helena's situation. Indeed, the Countess seems
to be testing Helena for the proper balance of frankness
and reserve, for a proper social piety in the service of
transgression, hence her close questioning. 'Had you not

lately an intent – speak truly –/To go to Paris?' The break commanding truth comes at just the rhetorically right point, after 'intent'. And the Countess's next question breaks so, rhythmically, again: 'Wherefore? tell true.' And again, after Helena speaks of the cure: 'This was your motive/For Paris was it? Speak.' Helena's reply is a positive masterpiece – of balanced evasiveness, some would say. 'My lord your son made me think of this;/Else Paris and the medicine and the King/Had from the conversation of my thoughts/Haply been absent.' Had Helena said less, denying *any* relation between her love of Bertram and the Paris trip, the Countess would have properly suspected a lie or hypocrisy. Had Helena said more, the Countess would have concluded that Helena was much too bold and calculating. Helena passes the test brilliantly: 'I will tell the truth, by grace itself I swear.' And so she does, perhaps.

Critics with a *parti pris* can argue that all this delicacy does not square with Helena's soliloquy at the end of the first scene of the play. There she seemed resolved to pursue Bertram actively, and she mentioned the King's disease in the same breath, and with only a change of grammatical direction between the two ideas. An actor confusing Helena with one of George Bernard Shaw's New Women propelled toward procreation by the Life Force can easily speak the soliloquy knowingly, as already having the whole plot in mind, and thus reply to the Countess with bland guile. Readers and audiences will have to judge whether the interpretation works. I do not think it fully responsive to the Helena of the text. The crucial difference is one between the deliberate manipulation of others to achieve an end one thinks can be brought about in no other way, and only striving to show one's merit, fully believing that in the nature of things that merit will somehow be rewarded: 'Who ever strove/To show her merit that did miss her love?' The distinction may well seem more tenuous or naïve now than it did when a kindly Creation was generally reckoned a probability. Determined schemers were no doubt as common on the seventeenth-century scene as they are today, but however one interprets Helena's soliloquy, one has to face the effort Shakespeare makes to forestall the impression that he is creating only an opportunist. Her self-questioning, it may be argued (incorrectly, I think), is hypocritical or self-deluding, but it is hard to interpret her long absence from the stage before her reappearance in Act 5 as other than an attempt to avoid showing us a Helena involved in more actual intrigue than is absolutely necessitated by the story.

Additionally, the actor-Countess may even be tempted to collaborate with Helena, deciding that the snatching of her son has 'raised the consciousness' of the Countess, thus making her willing to conspire with Helena to bring about the unmentionable alliance that will be the making of the boy. Both the meaning of the soliloquy and of the exchange between Helena and the Countess are left a bit open. But if a covertly conspiratorial Countess seems going too far, Helena's lack of a fully worked out scheme seems clear. 'Who ever strove/To show her merit that did miss her love?' Somehow, Helena thinks, merit will be rewarded. The 'luckiest stars in heaven' will sanctify the cure as 'my legacy'. The relation between love for Bertram and the curing of the King is left vaguely in the air, with providence or accident as a possible mediator. In the words of the Countess, Helena has indeed 'wound a goodly clew', put herself in a messy and difficult situation, but her control and modesty have shown her worthy, if not of success, at least of something even more rare – the help of a very proper lady in an enterprise that could lead to awkward consequences for her immediate family. The Countess's action in supporting Helena is in telling contrast to the support given Helena by the King. The Countess's support is freely given, without a *quid pro quo*, heartfelt, based on a profound sense of the merit of the recipient, and wholly unrhetorical. Finally, the King's help is a secular bargain; the Countess's help something of an act of piety. She will aid Helena in testing the judgement of providence.

Contemporary readers and audiences may find this strain of piety even more problematic than the play's social fabric. Yet Bertram really *desires* his mother's 'holy wishes', impolite though the timing of the request is. And the Countess in turn *means* it when she says 'Be thou blessed, Bertram.' Helena's love-imagery of 'idolatrous fancy' and relics to be sanctified is not mere ornament. It reflects a consciousness of the difference between the sacred and profane in love that plays no part in Giletta's thinking. The soliloquy in the first scene, which begins with Helena's declaration that 'Our remedies oft in ourselves do lie', does not counterpose initiative to divinity. Rather it is 'the fated sky' that 'Gives us free scope' and thwarts human effort only when initiative or deserving falters. In short, Heaven helps those who help themselves, if they are worthy. For Helena the Nature that will join like to like is not the Nature worshipped by Edmund in *King Lear*, a goddess at odds with divinity. When she replies to the Countess's warnings about the possible opposition to her cure from the College of Physicians, Helena says of her father's formula that 'There's something in it more than my father's skill', and that it 'Shall for my legacy be sanctified'.

The scene in which Helena proposes the cure is full of invocations of the spiritual. The introduction of rhymed couplets at II. i. 129 underscores the other-worldliness of the scene. Through several long speeches full of references to the deity, writ and miracles, Helena's argument is that the King's cure must be the work of heaven: 'Of heaven, not me, make an experiment.' We are never told Helena's medical procedure, but it is surely as extraordinary as its result. Giletta's plan goes forward in mechanical fashion; Shakespeare allows for an illusion of providential reward. In Boccaccio the King takes the initiative; in Shakespeare the King grants the initiative to Helena. The cure itself is announced in the next scene but one in Lafew's often-quoted speech:

> They say miracles are past; and we have our philosophi-
> cal persons to make modern [everyday] and familiar,
> things supernatural and causeless. Hence it is that we
> make trifles of terrors, ensconcing ourselves into seeming
> knowledge when we should submit ourselves to an
> unknown fear.
>
> (II. iii. 1–60)

The speech is a crystallisation of the allusions to providence
that cluster round Helena's curative powers and her further
progress, her fortuitously immediate encounter with the
Widow, for example.

This strain of the supernatural distinguishes *All's Well*
from its source; mentions of divinity in Boccaccio are
fleeting and bromidic. In *All's Well* the supernatural has
the effect of softening and deflecting Helena's activism
from calculating bustle to a more elevated risk-taking. If
the social gap between Bertram and Helena opened up by
Shakespeare's impoverishing her seems to cry out for
providential intervention, her appeal to it and indeed the
very idea of the providential in the play make it possible
to suggest a refinement of mind, at least a freedom from
bourgeois calculation that justifies her impoverishment as
a stroke of dramaturgy. Helena's Hamlet-like self-doubts
and self-accusations increase rather than lessen the effect.
More important, however, is the transformation in the
whole story effected by the presence of the supernatural.
Boccaccio's tale, for all its unusual bridging of class
disparity, is 'modern and familiar', 'ensconcing' us into
'seeming knowledge'. Once the force of love is set in
motion by habitual childhood proximity it is irresistible,
using any means as it moves toward its inevitable triumph.
That is not quite how Shakespeare wanted to tell his tale.
Complicating characters and obscuring motives (why *is*
Parolles obsessed with that drum?), Shakespeare creates a
world less easily reduced to a monolithic force that is the
sole cause of all effects. To say that 'all's well that ends

well' is to give up the pretence of predictable behaviour and outcome that follow from the seeming knowledge of secular law, and instead admit a variable, problematic fortune. For Helena, animated by love and trust in providence, all must end well, as it does with the King's cure. But Lafew is right in thinking that a commitment to secular rationalism tends to make (statistical?) trifles of terrors, and that rejecting it is a submission to an unknown fear, to forces beyond human understanding. This opens the possibility of some curious happy endings indeed.

An unknown fear seems precisely what Bertram faces in the highly theatrical scene in which he is chosen by Helena and cowed by the King. Helena's choice cannot be staged as it is told in Boccaccio, weightlessly brief and with Beltramo absent. As with the three caskets and the choice of Portia in *The Merchant of Venice*, the playwright stretches out the act of choosing, ritualises it for emphasis and gives us not only the act itself but commentators with opposite viewpoints.

The King's first words after entering, 'Go, call before me all the lords in court', suggest for a moment the breath-taking possibility that he will offer Helen every unwed courtier in the kingdom. The Folio stage direction reads – fortunately – 'Enter three or four lords.' 'This youthful parcel/Of noble bachelors stand at my bestowing,/O'er whom both sovereign power and father's voice/I have to use.' Here is power doubly derived, and perhaps a faint condescension. 'Parcel' is mostly used by Shakespeare of the inanimate or the small detail. When Portia speaks of 'a parcel of wooers' in *The Merchant of Venice* (I. ii. 97) she does so with tongue in cheek. 'Thou hast the power to choose,' the King tells Helena, 'and they none to forsake.' Helena deals graciously with the inevitable embarrassment of the situation by making a small joke. Lafew, however, greets the occasion with enthusiasm. There follows a small dancing out of what has already been decided. Helena approaches each of the four bachelor lords in turn, making a self-deprecatory and complimentary rhymed rejection of each until at last she comes to Bertram. Him she does not 'take'; rather she gives herself. Helena, despite her power, never forgets her social status.

How shall the scene be played? Joseph Price, one of the most acute commentators on the play, has ingeniously proposed (pp. 155–7) that we see the King's parcel of noble bachelors as far from enthusiastic about the possibility of marrying Helena: hence their laconic speech; hence Lafew's annoyance at them. Lafew, Price argues, 'vocalises our feelings [of sympathy] for Helena' and 'tempers our shock' by preparing us for Bertram's rejection. Why would a young courtier want such a marriage in any case?

With a director's ingenuity and an actor's expressiveness, almost anything may be done on stage. Their initial unison response to Helena's reference to the King's cure, 'We understand it, and thank heaven for you', has reduced the bachelor lords to royal cogs, as unison in *Hamlet* reduced Cornelius and Voltimand. This and their presence in the first instance is designed not only to give weight to the choice-scene, but to serve as concrete evidence of the King's power and to deny Bertram the possibility of special pleading. After their choral self-presentation, the First Lord speaks three words, the Second five, the Third nothing and the Fourth six. In one sense, it hardly matters whether the words are spoken with an intent to ingratiate the speakers with the King and so make a marriage that is bound to be attended by wealth and favour, or – though this would be more difficult for the actors – spoken in bitterness or anger between clenched teeth to convey their unwilling subjection to their royal guardian. If ingratiatingly, Lafew's annoyance can be made to seem directed at the brevity and hence apparently tepid enthusi-asm of their statements, an implied rebuke to manhood. If they speak reservedly or ironically, as Price would have them do, Lafew's anger (as before) is directed at a snobbish, milk-and-water generation that has neither ardent loyalty to the King nor a manly yen for a beautiful girl who has done a magnificent deed. Both stagings can convey the misfortunes of wardship and are consistent with the character of Lafew, who has entered the garrulous twilight of male potency. Either interpretation can prepare the way for Bertram's rejection of Helena. But the traditional interpretation is far easier to act, and so preferable. Playing the scene so that Lafew does not hear the young wards and thus misinterprets as rejection Helena's moving on from one to the other avoids the textual questions. How it would avoid audience confusion is hard to imagine. This, however, was Dr Johnson's suggestion. Yet why would Shakespeare have invented such a scene? Free-standing, Lafew's remarks would become a comic distraction occasioned by stage blocking whose one rationale is to permit them. They are significant only in relation to the speech of the wards, and not having Lafew hear them seems an unnecessary complication. Although the difficulty was apparently overcome in Tyrone Guthrie's 1959 production of *All's Well*, the effect was one of arbitrary comedy with no relevance to the rest of the scene. Willing or trapped, the wards bend to the King's power, and however they say it, nothing the wards say – for they say so little – will please Lafew. His enthusiasm and Helena's little dance of deferential eliminations heightens our expectation of Helena's choice. Perhaps the crucial problem in the scene for the director is Bertram. However the Lafew-ward relation is staged, the director is faced with slanting it so as to locate Bertram's rejection as either more courageous or more mean-spirited than the responses of the wards.

As Brian Parker has observed, the grounds on which Helena excuses the four young lords are precisely those that should also lead her to excuse Bertram. They suggest another basis for Bertram's conviction that he has been treated unjustly. Helena excuses the First Lord with only thanks for his willingness to hear (and grant) her suit. To the Second Lord she makes a difficult answer whose sense is that he is too high-born and deserves a fortune twenty times better. Helena promises the Third Lord that for his own sake she will never wrong him and hopes that he will find 'fairer fortune' if he weds. The Fourth Lord, she says, is too young, too happy, too good for her to marry. The main argument of Helena's kind dismissals is the difference in honour and fortune between herself and the lords. To overlook it, she says, would be a 'wrong'. Helena is clearly thinking of disparagement. Her other reasons: youth, happiness (good fortune), goodness – spoken to the Fourth Lord – are an odd mixture of the shrewd, the realistic and the idealising typical of Helena. Bertram does seem too young for any sort of intimate heterosexual bond; his circumstances are – or have been – too easy for his own good. Whether Bertram himself can be thought 'good' Helena will discover to her cost. Having given such strong reasons against doing so, Helena humbly offers herself to Bertram.

Bertram's outburst is unpleasant but not wholly unjustified. A plea to use his own eyes in choosing a wife would have found wide agreement in an Elizabethan audience, if not with parental peers of the realm. Romantic union was an idea gaining currency. That the King proposes to 'bring [Bertram] down' with his misalliance is also a valid objection. Bertram's disdain for a 'poor physician's daughter' who was a household dependant is another matter – a reasonable objection to some, vicious to a few. Shakespeare tips the balance and tries to direct judgement with the ironic last sentence of Bertram's speech: 'Disdain/Rather corrupt me ever!' The Arden editor reads this as 'I choose that my disdain of her should ruin my favour in your [the King's] sight rather than that I should be brought down by marriage to one beneath me.' As predictive irony the phrase is simpler, with Bertram choosing a snobbery that will set in train a course of self-destructive lies and deceptions. Perhaps he speaks more accurately than he knows.

The King's response to Bertram has been much admired as having 'a complex and bitter music' and expressing a humane and liberal outlook on the issues of class and power so obviously important in the play. The King states eloquently the commonplaces of the running argument over the relation between status and merit typical of deference societies: the irrelevance of status to essential humanity, the natural nobility of merit, the emptiness of rank without it, the likelihood of merit reproducing itself, the emptiness of ancestral title inherited without current merit. To these abstractions Bertram gives the heart's concrete answer, 'I cannot love her nor will strive to do it', and the King the only effective reply: 'My honour's at the stake . . ./I must produce my power.' Bertram sues for pardon.

The King's arguments are solid and reasonable. Who would deny them? Not one but has its counterpart in proverb and its illustration in social history. But upon inspection it appears that Shakespeare has made the solid slippery. Key terms are used too often for clarity: seven instances of 'honour' in some form; five of 'virtue'/ 'virtuous', each time employed somewhat differently, with virtue as a moral quality contending with virtue as power; honour as a moral quality contending with honour as title or respect given. And in the course of the King's attempt to redefine the idea of status he is forced to appeal to the axiom of identity, 'good alone is good; vileness is so', which makes definition futile. We know well enough what the King is saying: Helena is a marvel, worthy of all the terms of praise and acceptance going. But to say this when and how the King says it, and to whom he says it, is to call into question the validity of the whole apparatus of social distinctions he is trying to rationalise and renew by finding in them a place for Helena. Bertram's unmoved response reveals the arguments as misdirected to callowness, if not to the reason. The King, now livid, uses the word 'honour' twice again in ways that strip the camouflage from the others. When the King declares his honour at the stake he is speaking of his personal reputation (i.e. his claim to absoluteness in rule). To maintain it, he must

use his power, the power than enables him 'to plant thine
[Bertram's] honour where/We please to have it grow'.
The locution occurs again in *Macbeth* when King Duncan,
after loading him with praise and honour, tells Macbeth
'I have begun to plant thee, and will labour/To make thee
full of growing.' The whole apparatus of honour, revealed
by the logic of the narrative rather than by the logic of
argument, is that honour is, finally, what is bestowed by
the King in the course of maintaining his own status.
This narrative relation between the realities and the
rationalisations of power and status is neither inadvertent
nor merely a dividend from the Sonnets and the earlier
political plays. *All's Well* provides a fuller and more
detailed account of the character and limitations of power
and status. But here they are tellingly defined. Bertram
picks up the King's ultimate meaning of 'honour' and
appears to submit. 'When I consider/What great creation
and what dole of honour/Flies where you bid it,' Bertram
allows that Helena is to the manor born. Shakespeare
employs a splendidly outrageous pun. Of the six uses of
the word 'dole' in Shakespeare's plays five of them mean
extreme woe (dolour). Editors struggle with alternatives,
toy with an emendation to 'deal', but Bertram is right:
the King has given him a great misery of honour. Yet for
all his exercise of power, the King cannot quite marry
Bertram to Helena. Bertram refuses to consummate the
marriage.

Immediately afterward Bertram's resistance is played
out as comedy in Parolles' elaborately irritated denial of
Lafew's description of Bertram as Parolles' 'lord and
master'. 'Well, I must be patient' he says after Lafew
exits; 'there is no fettering of authority', and like Bertram
he resolves to have it his own way, were Lafew 'double
and double a lord'. When Bertram, now suddenly married,
re-enters, yet another camouflage meaning of 'honour'
reappears in Parolles' ribald assertion that 'He wears his
honour in a box unseen/That hugs his kicky-wicky here
at home,/Spending his manly marrow in her arms'.

Bertram agrees, and the two set off for the wars. There is no avoiding the sexual equations honour = penis, box = vagina after the reference to spent marrow. But should one attribute to the playwright a sexual ultimate at the core of the King's politically ultimate understanding of honour as the creation of power – an understanding of status as finally an expression of the gender-based and gender-nurtured system of power? Perhaps, but not on this evidence alone.

It is too congenial a reading of history to see the King's great speeches on the relation between merit and title only as reflections of the gradual weakening of deference and prerogative during the seventeenth century. Ironically, in the play they serve largely to further the exercise of arbitrary power. Yet the fiction is closer to the social actualities. Lawrence and Jeanne Stone conclude that until recently the English élite was just open enough to avoid violent opposition from merit absolutely denied, yet not so open to merit as to allow it systematically to supplant inherited privilege. The contradictions that unravel the King's speeches reflect the ideological difficulties of this long balancing-act of power.

The power of the King of France has enforced a marriage, but not quite. Even setting aside the issue of disparagement, Shakespeare's audiences would have recognised the questionable character of a marriage that violated the time-honoured legal doctrine of free consent. Though it, like disparagement, was a sufficient ground for the dissolution of a marriage, there is scant record of either ground having been effectively invoked. The sole example cited by Margaret Ranald in *Shakespeare and his Social Context* (1987), p. 246, is the annulment, on grounds of coercion, of the marriage of Consuelo Vanderbilt to the Duke of Marlborough, surely an instance of the convenience of legal archaeology. An Elizabethan audience would have recognised Helena's offering of herself to Bertram as a *de praesenti* spousal, Bertram's submissive 'I take her hand' as the gesture of 'handfasting' and consent and the King's reference to 'this contract' and to the 'ceremony' and 'solemn feast' as indicating a proper ratification of the public spousal *in facie ecclesiae*. Yet for all this the marriage is incomplete; it lacks not only the consummation, but even the nuptial kiss, which Bertram denies. Professor Ranald observes that according to Henry Swinburne's *Treatise of Spousals, or Matrimonial Contracts*, published in 1686, Bertram's abandonment of his bride before consummating it laid the basis for an escape from the marriage on the two grounds of coercion and prolonged absence. Even without this sort of information, audiences know well before the scene ends that royal authority has succeeded only in leading a colt to water. During the rest of the play the King acts as a passive observer of events or as Helena's unwitting instrument.

The King's sense of himself, hardly needed for the bare plot of *All's Well*, adds perspective to this picture of power exercised and undone. When Bertram first appears at the Court in the second scene of Act 1, the King greets him with the expected reflections on the valour and nobility of Bertram's father, reflections no doubt made embarrassing by the King's stated hopes of more than a physical resemblance in the son. These lead inevitably to the King's dark comments on his illness and on old age and to a wish that 'I quickly were dissolved from my hive/To give some labourers room'. The old metaphor is based on the Elizabethan error in assuming that the queen bee was a king and that more working bees can replace a queen. The Second Lord provides the obligatory response: 'You're loved, sir;/They that least lend it you shall lack you first.' The antecedent of 'it' is probably 'room' rather than 'love'. The Second Lord is saying that those who least acknowledge the King's usefulness (or, alternatively, least love him) will be the first to regret his absence. In any case, the significance of the exchange centres on the King's reply: 'I fill a place, I know it.' The tone of this is not in the abject, regretful vein of his rehearsal of old age and of the wisdom of Bertram's dead father. It is, however, quietly uttered, determined and assured; the two short clauses provide it with an emphatic rhythm. But this is not the affirmation or assurance of the ego. To fill up a place, here or in *As You Like It* (I. ii. 171–3) where the phrase is spoken by young Orlando, is to acknowledge one's self with some inevitable modesty as occupying a necessary slot – to use the military-administrative phrase – in the 'table of organization', presumably here the ordained scheme of the world.

In *All's Well* the word 'place' has a social meaning of office and status. The King had used it about thirty lines before in the sense of 'rank', and after his disastrous exposure as a coward the admirably resilient Parolles comforts himself with the thought that he will survive, indeed 'by foolery thrive', since 'There's place and means for every man alive'. Behind the King's assertion and Parolles' stands the common assumption of a Creation in which adequate provision has been made for all its creatures. 'I fill a place': I take up an assigned role; I act out its requirements. 'I know it': I know who I am; I affirm myself and my role by appropriate action. For all his illness and enervation the King of France is no self-indulgent Lear to shirk the pains of hereditary office and 'unburdened crawl toward death'. There is some point in remembering that he recovers an extraordinary vigour. At the end of the play, although he clearly recognises that he is old and that the 'noiseless foot of time' will come to steal his power, the King is not the sort to say with Prospero that every third thought will be his last.

The King of France is one of the more congenial of Shakespeare's royal creations. He does not complain of how uneasy his head lies because of a crown he has no intention of taking off; his arbitrary acts are at least translatable to non-political, human terms; his coercion of Bertram is unpleasant but finally ineffectual. Despite this last, the impression he makes over the whole of the play is one of modesty and conscientiousness coupled

with a royal presence and address – qualities rare enough
in the history plays, for example.

Yet there is something troubling about his conception
of an order wholly ordained; something dispiriting about
any decorum, literary or political, that has a place for
everything and puts everything in its place. It is enervating,
predictable, dull. *All's Well* seems trying to have things
both ways, insisting on the rightness of 'place', the stability
and orderliness of Rossillion and the Court, the pleasant
absence of significant issues of war or social order that
trouble other comedies. The Florentine war is far away
and empty; estate and court run smoothly. Yet the play
queries this model of orderliness by insisting on the vitality
and the place-jumping skills of Helena and Parolles, who
is described by Helena, in an often-quoted passage, as
having fixed (intractable) evils so appropriate that they
take 'place' when virtue seems too bleak for comfort. Is
Lafew's tame Parolles more properly in place than is the
wild Parolles, scarves flying, on the loose? Helen more
properly in place as Countess Helena than as Dr She or
the Purposeful Pilgrim? It is not only compression that
made Shakespeare's elimination of Giletta's successful
managerial career appropriate. The two most vital characters in the play – if nominally conformist – are total
outsiders. Rather than relief, the 'proper' placing of the
dis-placed, even of Bertram, adds an ironic effect to the
play's last moments.

There are two hierarchies of place in *All's Well*. The
first is an obvious secular social and political order; the
other a shadowy providential order, occasionally hinted
at, sometimes invoked, mischievously generous in its
allowance for Parolles, but clearly just in its elevation of
Helena. The second order is the ultimate validation of the
first – a substantial ideological convenience when the
conventional order must be modified in the face of
objections. But the problematic relation of the two orders
is suggestive of the historical moment as we see it, say,
in the history plays, where reason of state and divine

intent provide parallel but discontinuous lines of causation and meaning.

For the moment, however, it is useful to see the King of France as he sees himself: no Tamburlaine despite his bluster, rather a person bound by ideas of honour and convention, a servant of his place, exhibiting a few minor skills of governance, apparently unaware of his ineffectuality yet feeling himself a king whose 'quickest decrees' are now stolen by time before he can effect them. The King's modest self-conception matches the consistently undercut achievements of other characters in *All's Well*. At the same time, it permits audiences a sympathy that somewhat mitigates the effect of his coercion of Bertram.

If Bertram's flight shows the King's power to be limited, secular power in general is called further into question by Shakespeare's treatment of the Italian war. Shakespeare makes a speciality of wars for which it is difficult to work up any enthusiasm: wars initiated and sustained by arrogance and greed for power, and carefully emptied of meaningful justification. Even the national foundation wars of the English history plays, despite heroic moments – 'young Harry with his beaver on' – are presented by Shakespeare as a parade of inadequates on both sides in a bloody exchange of insecure power. Agincourt itself, its heroics largely encapsulated in *Henry V* by choruses, is bracketed by specious clerical rationalisation on one side and by Burgundy's picture of devastation and the Epilogue's dire recital of dynastic collapse on the other, the whole enterprise shadowed by Bolingbroke's advice to Henry to busy giddy minds with foreign quarrels. In *All's Well* Shakespeare goes beyond even the absurdity of the Polish 'egg-shell' for which Fortinbras is willing to risk 'the imminent death of twenty thousand men'.

Shakespeare uses deprecatory language in introducing the wars in the Problem Plays. In *Troilus and Cressida* the Prologue's word for the Trojan war is 'broils', its origins in 'vaunts' and 'firstlings'. In *All's Well* the King

introduces the Italian war by speaking of the Florentines
and Sienese in a casually deprecatory phrase: they 'are by
the ears', an allusion to fighting dogs. Apparently the two
sides are equally matched and continue 'a braving war', a
war of verbal challenges. On the advice of the Duke of
Austria, for some (not historical) reason the King's dearest
friend, France will deny Florence's expected plea for
support. For all this he freely allows any of his gentlemen
who wish to do so to fight in the war – on either side.
This curious advice and encouragement is explained by
the Second Lord: 'It well may serve/A nursery to our
gentry, who are sick/For breathing and exploit.' The idea
is a common one. Hamlet describes Fortinbras's invasion
of Poland as 'the imposthume [abscess] of much wealth
and peace,/That inward breaks, and shows no cause
without/Why the man dies'. Hamlet evidently mistakes
Fortinbras's motives, but correctly labels the result a
sickness. Running through *Henry V* is a tidal motif of
human, specifically male, pugnacity, 'wrangling' – an
inherent disposition to quarrel. The play is an encyclopedia
of wilful confrontations from Henry's invasion to assert
his supposed rights in France to Fluellen's battle to
vindicate the leek: war as genetically ordained. In Hamlet's
formulation it is as though the blockage of such pugnacity
had formed an abscess. But Hamlet's typically metaphysical
mode complicates the idea: the abscess breaks inwardly,
presumably infecting the mind. In *All's Well* the idea is
sociologised, the metaphor of illness made less sinister yet
apparently more extreme; the Italian wars are a training
ground (how ironic the word 'nursery' here!) for a warrior
class 'sick' for want of military action. Though this
mitigates the force of the suggestion of irremediable
pugnacity that one gets in *Henry V* and *Hamlet*, it retains
some of the perversity: 'sick' is perhaps too strong a term
for the desire to maintain professional military skills and
win renown, strong enough when the desire is for war.

    If anyone has missed the ludicrous implications of the
permission given the King's courtiers to fight on either

side, those implications are clarified at the outset of the second act. Here the King imparts military principles to two groups of young lords, bidding them share the advice, which is 'enough for both'. Even if his phrase 'if both gain all' – so difficult to place syntactically – means only 'if both groups profit fully from my advice' rather than 'if both groups are victorious', we are still looking at the interesting spectacle of the King telling his young courtiers how to behave properly in the course of killing one another.

The King's first speech indicates that his young noblemen are meant to come on stage in two groups and should probably leave in opposite direcitons, one group presumably for Florence, the other for Siena. Perhaps they intend to fight on alternate days to avoid fratricide; perhaps they agree to fight only on the left flank of their respective armies. But such specificity would have pushed into the zany what now can pass for the odd. Historical precedents of free lances fighting their countrymen in the cause of others do nothing to throw a colour of sobriety over the situation and staging Shakespeare has invented here. It is of a piece with the rest of the war: the remarkable elevation to the rank of cavalry general of the juvenile Bertram, who has gone to war to avoid a bridal-night; the rodomontade of Parolles and the delicious episode of the drum, and Bertram's incredible achievements – capturing Siena's greatest commander, slaying the duke's brother with his own hand. After the drum episode the war sinks almost without trace, its only memories in Lavatch's quip about Bertram's velvet patch, which may, he says, cover a battle scar or a venereal chancre; in Parolles' foul-smelling clothes, and in Bertram's accusation of Diana as 'a common gamester of the camp'. The only whiff of real powder we get is in Helena's evocative imagining of Bertram in danger from smoking muskets and leaden messengers (III.ii.108).

Shakespeare enhances the unlikeliness of the war by what we should recognize in film as adroit cutting. What cannot be 'motivated' or justified is presented *tout court*, suddenly and all at once, avoiding embarrassment, yet underlining the anomaly. Examples: sounds of trumpets and enter the Duke of Florence and his retinue, among them Bertram, last seen lying to his wife; first line: 'The general of our horse art thou.' Two scenes earlier: trumpets and enter the Duke of Florence with French Lords and soldiers; first lines: 'So that from point to point now have you heard/The fundamental reasons of this war.' The First French Lord finds the Florentine cause 'holy'; the Second can't say why the King of France will not support it, but the First is sure that young Frenchmen upset by peace will join up for the war-cure. Shakespeare jump-starts these scenes to avoid what cannot be explained and to call attention to the implausibility of the war. The effect is not one of fairy-tale unfolding but of social critique: the awkward moments of power-games, war without cause, command without experience or skill.

Nevertheless the apparently now phoney, braving war between the Sienese and the Florentines is a war that veterans of any war can believe in more readily than they can the heroics of Agincourt. Its unexpected authenticity on stage, however, rests almost entirely on Parolles' rhetoric, that extravagant, lying send-up of the commanders and the ranks, their equipment, their readiness, their morale – the universally denigrating 'griping' that is the (barely) acceptable displacement of the soldier's hatred of war and fearful disgust at his role in it. Parolles' language in betraying his friends and comrades has an authentic, heartfelt enthusiasm and a circumstantiality that smell of the bivouac. This is the Italian war: no Shrewsbury of hissing swords, no Agincourt of breach-filling. In *All's Well* the corrosive Falstaffian estimate of war has no opposing vision. Underneath it here and in Shakespeare's other plays lie report and reflection, the scepticism of the Sonnets and perhaps a recollection of the Erasmian humanist reaction to the continental wars of Henry VIII.

Yet there is more to Shakespeare's Tuscan war than

anti-war perspectives. The young noblemen of France have not *all* run off to Italy to escape their wives or to improve their professional skills. 'These balls bound; there's noise in it', cries Parolles. 'O, 'tis brave wars!' says the Second Lord. Twin motives of the prospective warriors are adventure and the 'honour [to] be bought'. There is so much honour indeed that when Bertram – before Helena's choice is even dreamt of – proposes to defy the King's orders and 'steal away' to war (II.i.33), the First Lord tells him that 'There's honour in the theft' and the Second offers to be Bertram's 'accessary'. The young gentlemen 'wear themselves in the cap of the time; . . . eat, speak, and move under the influence of the most received star; and though the devil lead the measure, such are to be followed'. War, in short, is the done thing, according to Parolles, whatever the auspices – Florentine, Sienese or infernal. To this triad of adventure, honour and fashion (the cant virtue of 'sharing the experience of one's own generation'), the King adds an equivocating fourth. If the French 'lack language to deny' when 'Those girls of Italy' demand, the warning to 'take heed of them' is half invitation. It also specifies how Bertram will capitulate to Diana's demand for his precious ring.

Bertram's victories are treated perfunctorily – unless one takes the stage directions literally and allows Bertram, Parolles *and the whole army* to pass over the stage in glory in Act 3 Scene 5. But the queries of Helena about Bertram and Parolles and the sharp replies of Diana darken the occasion. 'Marry, hang you!' and 'ring-carrier!' the women call as the parade exits. The sole staged action of the Tuscan war is Parolles' adventure of the drum, in the course of which his cowardice is revealed. The episode serves to deflect attention from Helena's questionable intrigue, to enlighten Bertram and to foretell and parallel *his* exposure, to set us thinking of the implications of Parolles' query 'Who cannot be crushed with a plot?' and finally and most obviously to provide a delightful and impudent entertainment. Yet for all the importance of its

other functions, the unmasking of Parolles furthers the
dissection of 'honour' begun earlier and applies its
implications to the examination of power and war.

Apparently a Florentine company drum had been
captured by the Sienese during a skirmish the Florentines
ultimately won. Parolles, ever solicitous of the honour of
his company, proposes to retrieve it single-handed. The
drum obsesses him. Well it might, since it was lost in 'a
disaster of war', but one the Second Lord thinks that
'Caesar himself could not have prevented if he had been
there to command'. That this should be the particular
disaster is emblematic of this braving war in which
Frenchmen go at one another for honour and exercise. It
occurred because the Florentines had made a cavalry attack
on their own flanks. Bertram's 'Well, we cannot greatly
condemn our success', shows his precocious mastery of
the explanatory style of war dispatches. But the loss of
the drum still troubles Parolles. He is determined to
recover it and is mischievously encouraged to do so by
the young lords, who are plotting to expose Parolles by
disguising themselves as the Sienese enemy, capturing
Parolles in the course of his mission and frightening him
into betraying his comrades. Needless to say, this attack,
once again on their own man, also succeeds.

In the drum itself, alternately 'but a drum' and an
'instrument of honour', Shakespeare has found a rich icon
at once signifying Parolles, war and honour. Empty, and
loud because it is empty, associated with Mars (III.iii.11)
and with a good beating ('John Drum's entertainment',
III.iii.36-7), the drum controls the rhythm of march,
conveys the order to advance or retreat – altogether a fine
object for martial respect. In addition, the drum is
significantly referred to as announcing the appearance of
troupes of strolling players.

For this symbol Parolles proposes to enter a no man's
land – or pretend to do so – and expose himself to danger
for a task that his betters have judged impossible and
unnecessary. Not only that, but any ruse he invents must

be 'very plausive' since Parolles thinks that he is already under some suspicion. 'What the devil should move me to undertake the recovery of this drum, being not ignorant of the impossibility, and knowing that I had no such purpose?' Parolles asks the question we have all been asking. He attempts to answer it just before his mock-enemies are to declare his doom. His motives, so he tells us, are 'Only to seem to deserve well and to beguile the suppositions of that lascivious young boy, the count', he says 'have I run into this danger; yet who would have suspected an ambush where I was taken?'

In a general way the answer is correct: for the sake of continued patronage. It is an answer that will cover a questioning of any of Parolles' actions, and one that Iago might offer with as much colour of truth, and as much superficiality. The answer is at once too broad and too limited. It does not answer the narrow question, yes, but why the drum? or the wider one, yes, but why the rhetorical and intriguing virtuosity, the dramatising impulse of 'Tongue, I must put you into a butter-woman's mouth . . . if you prattle me into these perils' (IV.i.41–3). Clearly Monsieur Words sees his tongue as autonomous, his rhetoric as something apart from himself, going off to lead its own life at peril of his. The broad answer to the question is perhaps that Parolles went after the drum because he was victimised by his own rhetoric, here the rhetoric of honour and military exploit. While his very name tells us that his author expected us to take such victimisation as in part an emblematic psychological phenomenon, it is unlikely that we are meant to see Parolles as only a freak *sui generis*. First of all, Parolles is appreciated: 'I begin to love him for this', says the First Lord after one of Parolles' virtuoso catalogues of insulting lies about the First Lord himself. When Parolles continues, reducing the First Lord's military expertness to leading a drum in front of touring actors, the First Lord is ecstatic: 'He hath out-villained villainy so far that the rarity redeems him' (IV.iii.264–5). The allusion to the drum as the herald of theatrical entertainment comes at precisely the right moment. What the First Lord praises is Parolles as theatrical entertainer, perhaps in the vein of extravagant theatricality that Hamlet rejects for out-Heroding Herod, but theatricality none the less in its surreal representation of character-types as amusing performances that mitigate the dangers they represent in 'real' life. Certainly Parolles constitutes no threat except to the wholly gullible, like Bertram, who might trust him with military responsibilities.

There is an important connection between the First Lord's liking for Parolles as liar, Helena's characterising of him as a marvellous scoundrel in the first act and the First Lord's earlier query about Parolles: 'Is it possible he should know what he is, and be that he is?' (IV.i.44–5). Not only is it possible, but perhaps necessary. Parolles is completely Parolles. His self-knowledge is insulated from his behaviour and no change in him is possible. Nor would one want any. What is 'fixed in him' may be 'evils' – though this word of Helena's seems too strong and prim for the actual Parolles – but his 'evils' have a stage perfection that makes him a rarity, something to be collected and admired as in a curio cabinet. It is this quality of amusing rascality that has resulted in the comparison of Parolles with Falstaff. The comparison is apt but needs qualification. Parolles is a social climber; Falstaff – more formally Sir John – needs no class elevation; he is merely an opportunist. The significance of this distinction is that for all his extravagant lies about his fellow officers, what Parolles wants as he climbs the greased pole is social acceptance. He preens himself before Helena on his going to court. Yet even though he is, as Lafew tells him, 'more saucy with lords and honourable personages' than his birth and virtue give him warrant, Parolles knows his place. 'Well, I must be patient; there is no fettering of authority' (II.iii.233). Falstaff has no such place to gain or limits to respect. Falstaff's attack on 'honour' and military prowess is direct, and mordantly

rational. Parolles does not attack either. Pretending to
exemplify them, he calls them into question through
trivialisation. If he exploits them or rather the idea of
them, he is also their victim. This last is the broad answer
to the question of why he undertakes the impossible and
useless exploit of the drum. Like all the French volunteers,
and probably the Florentines and Sienese as well (since
other motives are precluded by Shakespeare's calling
attention to their omission and vagueness), even the
cowardly Parolles is trapped in the rhetoric of honour.
He must be seen to do what others do because it is the
done thing, and thus generates the idea of a value that
supposedly justifies its doing. This is not to say that
honour is suspect because a coward pretends to it. Rather,
the mechanisms of emulation and entangling rhetoric
which sustain military honour in *All's Well* are reduced
in Parolles to an absurdity. Absurdity lurks also in the
deliberately omitted justifications for the Italian war, in
the volunteering of the French for *both* sides, in the
Florentine attack on their own men and in the symbolism
of the drum.

The conclusion of the war, if that is what it is, is more
peculiar still. In Act 4 Scene 4, Helena tells the widow
that 'The army breaking,/My husband hies him home
. . .'. 'Breaking' here means disbanding. Was the army
withdrawing for the winter? Had the Florentines won?
Coming immediately after Parolles' betrayal of the Florentines, with its circumstantial account of military matters
of immediate use to the enemy, disbanding, withdrawal
or victory seem equally illogical and unprepared for. The
war ends simply as a theatrical convenience; it is time for
Bertram to return to Rossillion.

Parolles' war is significantly interwoven with Bertram's
wooing. The conquest of Diana, in the event as delusory
as Parolles' quest for the drum, is conducted in scenes
that alternate with the Parolles farce. Connections are
evidently intended. Bertram too is trapped in the popular
rhetoric, uttering the conventional oaths, but having to

validate them by actually giving away the ring that represents 'My house, mine honour'. After he leaves, Diana reflects on the scene:

> My mother told me just how he would woo
> As if she sat in his heart. She says all men
> Have the like oaths.

(IV.ii.69–70)

The predictable rhetorics of honour and seduction deepen the impression of the narrow courses of human action, the extent to which both Parolles and Bertram, and by implication others, merely 'wear themselves in the cap of the time . . . under the influence of the most received star' (II.i.51–4).

Honour is variously birth, virtue, reputation, power, what the King will, the done thing – defended in some guises, criticised in others, and also mocked. Parolles' treading on the language of Lafew's enthusiasm after the King's cure (II.iii.1 ff.) is mocking and impudent, but directed more at Lafew's age and presumed old-fashioned attitudes than at his status, although there is, as Lafew later points out, a place-jumping element in it. Another amusing bit of mockery, aimed at the Court and specifically at ideas of status and deference, is Lavatch's fine fooling with the Countess in Act 2 Scene 2. It serves logistically to intervene between Helena's promise of a cure and the discussion of her miraculous success, but it is far from the vulgar and irrelevant filler it is sometimes taken to be.

Before Lavatch is to be sent to the Court with a letter to Helena and greetings to Bertram and others, the Countess proposes to examine him on the state of courtly manners. His first courtly response is to scorn the Court. The Countess's query 'What place do you think is truly important if you speak of the Court with such contempt' (II.ii.5–6) is not answered directly, but it is an embossed invitation to Lavatch to perform as a 'thoughtful clown'. Lavatch reduces the obligatory courtly skills to a leg bent, a cap doffed, a hand kissed and a mouth kept shut. But

Lavatch's particular accomplishments go beyond these: 'I have an answer will serve all men' as 'a barber's chair fits all buttocks'. Not only will it serve all men, it will, as the Countess elicits from Lavatch, 'serve fit to all questions', as fit as – and there follows a series of mocking comparisons that reflect no good on attorneys, whores, rustic lovers, cuckolds, shrews and clerics. Lavatch's almost universally appropriate response – fit for and to 'From below your duke to beneath your constable' – is 'O Lord, sir!' The Countess puts Lavatch and his verbal panacea to the test and both pass all her hypothetical situations save the possibility of a whipping for Lavatch himself. Realistic as he is, Lavatch concludes that 'things may serve long, but not serve ever'.

Lavatch's 'O Lord, sir!' is a phrase used four times in *Love's Labour's Lost*, twice in Marston's *Dutch Courtesan*, and in both Jonson's *Every Man Out of his Honour* and his *Cynthia's Revels*, always as a polite and fashionable way of sustaining conversation while saying nothing. In *All's Well* it still says nothing, but it does mean something. The phrase consists of an interjection that gives moment, an air of surprise, dismay, enlightenment or mere intensity, to what follows, and what follows are two conventionally deferential references. The phrase says nothing, but in a substantive way; it is the cachet of submissiveness. No difficulty is to be expected from the pious and thoroughly tame forelock-tugger who utters this phrase, which is the password for entry into the socially armed camp of deference, court society.

Lavatch's exchange with the Countess is sadly similar in construction to the King's coercion of Bertram and Parolles' mocking of Lafew after the King's cure. In all three scenes, after some foreplay, finally the social superior brings out *force majeure* and the game of statement and response is over. The King says that he must produce his 'power', Parolles acknowledges that 'there is no fettering of authority' and the mild Countess invokes for Lavatch the memory of a whipping. Lavatch is forced to acknowledge that even the obsequious defence of 'O Lord, sir!', though it may serve long, cannot serve ever. The clever skit between the Countess and Lavatch – which turns on the import of an apparently popular saying – gives us the life of privilege at court as a confrontation of ranks that empties verbal exchange of all but expressions of deference, which nevertheless fail to prevent the inevitable unpleasant coercion. Perhaps the Countess's 'You were lately whipped, sir, as I think' (II.ii.46) is a test-question only, not a reference to an actual event at Rossillion. One hopes so. But in asking it, even the gentle Countess shows that she knows Lavatch's place as well as he does. The mockery of deference and of those who practise it is proper to a thoughtful clown, but somewhat bitter. His experience of the Court makes Lavatch consider himself now beyond even the bleak enjoyment of Isbel.

Elsewhere, too, Lavatch is Shakespeare's vehicle for mockery. Speaking to Lafew in Act 4 Scene 5, he equates the heroic Black Prince with 'the prince of darkness alias the devil', who is surely 'the prince of the world'. Lavatch bids 'his nobility remain in his court', presumably hell, which Lavatch hopes to avoid, though 'pomp' will take the wider gate to 'the great fire'. Lafew, who had just given Lavatch a purse for his cleverness, is suddenly unamused ('I begin to be aweary with thee') and dismisses Lavatch with an order to see that his horses are taken care of, and 'without any tricks' (IV.v.39–56). When the Countess apologises for her shrewd (biting) and unhappy (sharp) servant, Lafew graciously lets the matter drop: 'I like him well; 'tis not amiss.' When Lavatch re-enters, he brings news of Bertram's return, offering a rude explanation (a syphilis scar) of the velvet patch on Bertram's left cheek and describing the men with Bertram as having 'delicate fine hats, and most courteous feathers which bow the head and not at every man'. Even feathers have apparently picked up the trick of saying 'O Lord, sir'.

The witty mocking and critique of authority was the stock-in-trade of Elizabethan theatrical clowns and Lavatch is no exception. But his mockery is sharp and precisely focused, and has a consistent thematic relevance. Lavatch brings to the play a negation of official culture, a reminder of the material and the bodily, and with them a spirit of frankness and familiarity. But one must stop short of Bakhtin's caveat in *Rabelais and his World* against finding such figures as Lavatch satiric. The corrosive quality of the play is not restricted to opportune by the by verbal jabs. Its whole structure is ironic. Orders enforced, aims achieved, prowess displayed – all somehow end unsatisfactorily.

The novelist George Meredith thought comedy women's best friend; *All's Well* illustrates the proposition. In the tragedies and histories women are largely victims. But in the comedies the triumphs of men require the triumphs of women, and comedy's founding of new social harmonies cannot take place without them. For the most part, however, women are denied nominal power and high status in *All's Well*. Even the Countess's rank cannot keep her son at Rossillion or living with Helena. Helena's cure of the King gives her a power (provided ultimately, one assumes, by heaven) that is wholly outside social convention. The women in *All's Well* have in some sense fallen on evil times, the Countess through isolation, and Helena, the Widow and Diana are all 'gentler' than their circumstances. Yet it is the mutual aid of these women, victimised or deprived in various ways, that achieves what the King cannot bring about and what Bertram went to war rather than face. This is the reverse side of Shakespeare's picture of power and status.

It is too easy to imagine as merely sentimental or moral categories the male-dominated world of power and status, with its dangerous ineffectualities and all too mockable pretensions, and in contrast the network of women joined together by mutual concern who manage rather easily to reduce the men of the play to bemused accessories. Yet for all that, the King is admirably conscientious, Lafew amusing, perceptive and sympathetic, the Dumain brothers not only zealous in exposing Parolles, but decent and thoughtful in their dismay at Bertram as seducer.

Whether the women of *All's Well* exhibit a similar even-handed complexity is a question for later discussion. But is is appropriate now to say something about their power and status. Although the network of Helena and her allies achieves its aim in the face of great odds, their 'power' is directed to only a narrow, particular goal, and one which itself imposes powerlessness. For all Helena's resolve and initiative in the courtship and consummation, the marriage itself is represented in the play as a yoke of male domination.

Only the fact that the Countess is widowed makes it possible for her to help Helena so easily. Only the fact that both Helena and Diana are fatherless permits them a latitude in behaviour that, say, Lafew's daughter Maudlin would not have. Lafew will settle Maudlin on Bertram, or, when Bertram is exposed, buy her a son-in-law at a fair. In contrast, Helena and Diana earn and are offered choices, subject, however, to proofs of their virginity – to which there is no father's word to be readily accepted as testimony. The King's cure validates Helena's virginity; Diana's is made one subject in the series of conditional 'If' statements (three of them having to do with the 'honesty' of women) that ends the play.

The Maudlin–Bertram match is instructive. Lafew asks the Countess if she approves of it, but only *after* he has contrived to have the King 'propose' it 'out of a self-gracious remembrance'. The King 'hath promised me to do it', says Lafew, the promise resting of course on the fact of the minority of both Bertram and Maudlin. This exchange of gracious agreement does not conceal the inequalities of gender. Later in the scene the King asks Lafew, 'What says he to your daughter?', and when told that this time Bertram accepts his authority, the King says 'Then shall we have a match', and later, 'The main consents are had' (V.iii.69). Maudlin is not consulted; the Countess consulted only after the fact.

Marriage itself demanded continued submissiveness. The classic text, employed with 'damnable iteration' in tract and sermon, was Ephesians 5:22, in which Paul cautioned, 'Wives, submit yourselves unto your husbands, as unto the Lord.' In law and in social theory a wife was, as one writer put it, '*quodammodo* an infant'. That Englishwomen were widely thought the freest in Europe suggests – if other evidence than common sense were needed – that not every Elizabethan wife practised the deadly virtues extolled in the conduct books. Typically, the married women in Shakespeare's comedies are restive under the yoke, and ultimately achieve a measure of freedom behind a translucent, if not transparent, screen of public conformity. For all that, there is no suggestion that the full implications of independence and mutuality suggested in the ideas and behaviour of some of his witty women in love – Beatrice in *Much Ado*, for example – will be realised in the stage marriages that end the comedies. The conundrum conformity of Kate at the end of *The Taming of the Shrew* is perhaps all that is to be hoped for. If marriage is seen as a compromise, it is not only a compromise of the sexes, but a compromise with the conventions.

There is none of this in *All's Well*. It offers not a compromise but a surrender to convention. Helena's love-combat is entirely against herself in soliloquy; her expression of independence is the lonely intrigue leading to the cure or the consummation. In choosing Bertram she seems to have learned her Ephesians by heart:

> I dare not say I take you, but I give
> Me and my service ever whilst I live,
> Into your guiding power. This is the man.
>
> (III.iii.102–4)

It all can be read as orthodox until the rhythm breaks in the last line with the laconically direct language of the police line-up. The passage inverts the order of romantic comedy and exaggerates its substance: the power of women in courtship; their powerlessness in marriage. On stage, Helenas typically speak 'This is the man' with the same quiet reverentiality as the preceding passage of submission, emphasising its difference from the modest, slightly arch levity of Helena's earlier avoidance of the young wards. In the stage moment, however, we are sharply aware of the theatrical contrast between Helena's abject submission in marriage and her actual power in this one choice, a contrast that further emphasises the submission. From this point on Helena's conduct is as orthodox and exemplary as patient Griselda's; she accepts all of Bertram's frigid meanness, obeys his commands to the letter (thereby, however, defeating their spirit) and finally reappears in the fifth act in Rossillion, still the traditional wife. When the King asks if Helena – supposedly dead – is a spirit or a reality, she replies,

> 'Tis but the shadow of a wife you see;
> The name and not the thing.

(V.iii.301–2)

This pregnant shadow-Helena can remind Bertram of the bed-trick not only without rancour, but even with pleasure: 'I thought you wondrous kind.' What will make her the substance rather than the shadow of a wife, however, is Bertram's approval, which is grudgingly and only conditionally given. Legally, Helena is correct to a nicety. The marriage has been consummated, but there are still technically the lingering legal questions of 'reverential fear' and moral compulsion by a guardian. These can be removed only by Bertram's free consent; technically he still withholds it. The stage spectacle, however, is bizarre. Helena, sufficiently along in her pregnancy (about four or five months) to feel 'her young one kick', speaks of herself as only the shadow of a wife. If we are to believe the words of the Beadle in Act 5 Scene 4 of *2 Henry IV*, pregnancy on stage was suggested by puffing out the costume with cushions. This Helena would have been a most substantial shadow. Perhaps this most peculiar courtship in Shakespeare has resulted, for all its vicissitudes, in what may be his most conventional marriage.

Wed or wooing, Helena is as submissive in speech as any preacher could require. It is not incorrect to think she might alter after the play ends – only irrelevant. The impression of the powerlessness of women, their lack of any claim apart from what submissiveness gives them, is further reinforced in the final scene of the play by the analogous situations of Maudlin and Diana, the one to be coaxed by a sparkling gift and married off as per agreement between her father and the King, the other to be 'rewarded' with marriage should she be demonstrably still a virgin.

According to some interpreters of the play, submissive is precisely the wrong adjective to apply to Helena. The Helena they see is an activist Helena, an emancipated woman driven by the Life Force, or – alternatively – a scheming hypocrite and 'huntress of men' driven by mean ambition and 'desperate sexuality'. The bare plot of *All's Well* can accommodate such views and still further nuances that depend on the varieties of hypothetical Bertrams (fearfully pubescent, merely vicious, half-victim and half-baked). Certainly actors are capable of 'projecting' such Helenas and Bertrams and clever directors can place the appropriate emphasis on scenes to support such views and further strengthen the interpretation by snipping out non-conforming bits of text. A variety of such interpretations can make for exciting theatre, and uncover potentialities of the text. Shakespeare's scripts are closer to actuality than they are to comments on actuality. They offer concrete details open to many inferences rather than narrow implications to be accepted without question. Hence there is generally some unperformable openness in his scripts which directors and actors must forgo since neither a Helena nor any other complex figure can be all things at once. Readers and critics, however, cannot feel under a similar restriction, and so may preserve and comment, even equivocally, on the unactable ambiguities and apparently contradictory meanings of the play-script. Despite this there are limits to all but admittedly wilful interpretations. Many of these are imposed by the conditions of language and thought when the work was written. Both Shaw's New Woman and Sir E. K. Chambers's 'huntress of men' are redolent of the early decades of this century, and the complex love-hate relationship of such critics to the emerging movements for women's rights.

The sparkle of relevance, however, can obscure the language and substance of the play, which derive from their connectedness through the particular historical moment of their creation. Whatever the concern of readers and critics for intended or authors' meanings, performers must of necessity take into account the now current relevance of plays, not only for its attractive sparkle but because the relevance of the play is the screen of preconception through which audiences see it. Perhaps nothing in *All's Well* is so immediately relevant as its representation of gender and sexuality.

· 4 ·

Gender and Sexuality

I must say Helena is a terrifying female. Her virtue, her persistence, her pegging away at the odious Bertram (and disguised as a pilgrim – so typical!) and then telling the whole story to that *good* widow-woman! And that tame fish Diana. As to lying in Diana's bed and enjoying the embraces meant for Diana – well, I know nothing more sickening. It would take a respectable woman to do such a thing. The worst of it is I can so well imagine . . . for instance acting in precisely that way, and giving Diana a present afterwards. *What* a cup of tea the Widow and D must have enjoyed while it was taking place, or did D at the last moment want to cry off the bargain? But to forgive such a woman! Yet Bertram would. There's an espèce de mothers-boyisme in him which makes him stupid enough for anything.

Unfair and extreme as this reaction to Helena is, one knows what Katherine Mansfield meant by it; this is the prosecution's case from the feminist side. Helena's unswervingly correct behaviour and single-mindedness, kept honour-bright by self-questioning and humiliation, seemed to Mansfield unforgiveable. She saw Helena accepting without protest the demeaning terms of an oppressive society, making that acceptance the basis of her respectability and knowing just how to use that respectability to get what she wanted. And what *did* she want? Bertram, a very noble and thoroughly impossible creature. Is this what virtue and devotion are for? If Helena lacks humanising flaws, she also lacks the qualities that make for genuine human strength: a commitment to dignity and self-respect, even a commitment to her own emotional needs. Any of these would have precluded Helena's arrangement of the bed-trick, let alone her enjoying it. For Mansfield it is not self-sacrifice in some praiseworthy sense that society requires before it stamps women respectable, but a total sacrifice of Self, an abandonment of dignity.

Helena's co-conspirators, Mansfield thinks, are not much better. Diana lends her name to a sordid cheat, and possibly has a self-righteous gossip (or is it a good laugh?) about it over tea with her mother. Mansfield even attributes Bertram's forgiveness of Helena (that is what Mansfield thinks it) to a childish need for maternal approval inculcated by the Countess. Mansfield's anger is directed at almost all the women in the play, and also at one other woman, the unwritten Myself lurking behind the three dots indicating a syntactical shift that slightly generalises to all women the burden of guilt, here the burden of conformism verging on hypocrisy.

Mansfield's comment on Bertram's 'mothers-boyisme' is more accurate historically than she may have known. Children of the early 1600s were routinely expected to pay their parents extraordinary outward marks of deference; John Donne thought this display unique in Europe. And though Bertram, like the polite Laertes, desires a parent's blessing on his departure, his maladroit interruption of her conversation brings down a smart rebuke from Lafew. Though the Countess certainly exposed Bertram to prayer and instruction, evidently she had spared him the routine floggings that were intended to achieve the aim of early seventeenth-century childhood education: breaking the child's will. (Shakespeare returned to the

problem of another fatherless, mis-educated and immature
military *Wunderkind* in *Coriolanus*.)

But for all their perceptiveness, Mansfield's views of
Helena, even of Bertram, are not quite fair. They deal
with only part of Helena, and Helena is herself only a
'part' whose whole, the play, must rightly bear the burden
of any gender-directed criticism. Mansfield's notes on
All's Well, written late in 1921, emerge from the same
ambience as the comments of E. K. Chambers and Shaw:
the atmosphere of challenge to social orthodoxy prompted
by the disillusion following the First World War, and the
nostalgic efforts to restore that orthodoxy. Yet Mansfield's
evolving belief that the conventionally feminine, like the
radically feminist, was essentially learned or imposed by
society on women suggests she might have reached at
some point a more charitable view of Helena. Some of
Mansfield's anger is, in any case, self-directed, a disgust
at her own susceptibility to a conformity to repugnant
values that had become an insidious second nature.

About some aspects of Helena, the abject quality of her
love, for example, Mansfield is agreeably up-to-date.
Hardly anyone now seems ready to accept the view that
in her unswerving devotion Helena was Shakespeare's
'loveliest creation' (Coleridge), or that she is distinguished
by a triumphant 'beauty of character' (Anna Jameson).
But like these nineteenth-century critics, Mansfield seems
to be judging Helena by the standards of a later age. Yet
this way of dissenting from Mansfield's views is itself not
quite fair. For all the changes in the situation of women
between the first decade of the seventeenth century and
the second decade of the twentieth, enough of the old
imperatives and expectations remained to make Helena
for Katherine Mansfield an infuriating reminder of their
persistence. It is still the case that attempts at the historical
'recovery' of Helena dredge up much of the present.

In a textually confused and difficult passage in the first
scene, the Countess praises Helena and expresses 'hopes
of her good that her education promises'. Not, surely,

education as we think of it now. The New Cambridge (1985) gloss equates 'education' here with 'upbringing', which is closer to the Shakespearian meaning but not quite full enough. The Countess's speech ends with: '. . . she derives her honesty and achieves her goodness' (I.i.36–42). This alludes to the nature of the education then generally thought proper for young women, an education designed primarily to preserve and refine female modesty.

Modesty, with its more pointedly sexual companion-term 'honesty', was the early seventeenth-century equivalent of Katherine Mansfield's detestable feminine respectability. The difference between 'respectability' and words like 'modesty' and 'honesty' is that while it focuses on the importance of social approval and surveillance, it veils more completely the core idea frankly expressed in the word 'impudence', not as now merely a breach of manners, but as understood at the time of *All's Well*. When asked by the King what she is willing to risk if he allows her to attempt the cure, Helena replies:

> Tax of impudence,
> A strumpet's boldness, a divulged shame,
> Traduced by odious ballads; my maiden's name
> Seared otherwise; ne worse of worst, extended
> With vilest torture, let my life be ended.
>
> (II.i.169–73)

Far from being the culminating punishment, the forfeiture of life after torture is only a comparative 'worse' after the 'worst'. Death on the rack is an anti-climax after the death of sexual honour. 'Impudence', whose meaning has now dwindled in force and relevance, is related etymologically to the genitalia (*pudenda*). Helen's repetitions make the point clearly. She is risking 'a fate worse than death'.

Shakespeare's fictional Helena, conventional in so many other ways, was in at least one respect unrepresentative of women at the time the play was written. Whether Shakespeare's daughter Judith could as much as sign her own name is a disputed question. It is going too far to

link Helena with Miranda of *The Tempest* as have some
recent scholars. She is not her father's apprentice, not the
recipient of a long schooling in medicine. She has some
medical formulas given to her on her father's death-bed,
but she has no pretensions to being in fact Dr She, the
learned medical amateur or the village wisewoman. When
the Countess asks her how the King and his physicians
can be expected to believe 'a poor unlearned virgin' when
they have exhausted all their proper medical knowledge
and failed, Helena does not protest her superior learning,
nor even her father's. But she does claim or at least hope
for the aid of 'something' more, the blessing of 'the
luckiest stars in heaven' on her father's 'good receipt'.

Despite her daring initiative, it is Helena's conventionality that Shakespeare is insisting on. She is no Renaissance
bluestocking, meddling in learning. That was the proper
sphere of men; Helena depends on providence. After a
few decades in the mid-sixteenth century when the bias
against intellectual women had lessened, the Learned Lady
had once again become a social misfit, 'a comet that bodes
mischief whenever it appears'. There were of course
exceptions, notably Queen Elizabeth herself. But this was
understandable, not merely because a taste for books as
for anything else was a privilege of majesty, but because
knowledge was, or was thought to be, easily converted
to power. Book-learning was subversive of women's
modesty and lowly station since its power could lead to
false pride and contentiousness, and to a dependence on
reason (in any case supposed to be naturally weak in
women), rather than on men and on religion. Shakespeare
is scrupulous in giving us what at first glance appears to
be a conventional Helena: unlearned, modest and pious.

But he obviously gives us more than this – a Helena
who can talk (or at least listen to) smut with Parolles,
aspire to lose her virginity to her own liking, set in motion
the intrigue that enables her to complete the impossible
tasks Bertram has imposed on her, and finally stage-
manage his painful exposure and recapture at the end of

the play. What to make of these 'two Helenas' is perhaps still the thorniest critical question of the play. It continually troubles actors, critics and audiences alike, evidently troubled Shakespeare and, in another sense, troubled even Helena, who offers at crucial moments to retreat from her actions and apologise for her feelings.

Shakespeare's Helena has probably 'read' her critics at least as effectively as they have read her. According to their time, outlook and sex, critics have responded with anger or adulation to her patient subservience; with disgust, fear or grudging respect to her single-mindedness and success. The critical response to Helena is an anthology of (largely male) thinking about the status of women. It is testimony to the richness of the character and to the force and variety of stage interpretations – as well as to the partisanship which the unsettled question of the status of women encourages – that critical discussions of Helena seem so partial and unsatisfactory. In what is arguably the most balanced, and certainly the most congenial, short study of *All's Well*, A. P. Rossiter insisted several times that the analysis of Helena's character can only result in confusion.

> I take her for granted which is the right way with her . . . for if you analyse her, you find that her only *noble* qualities are courage and the Stoical reserve which can take a blow with dignity and few words. The rest of her qualities are: a possessive passion for her man; an unconquerable determination (which one man will ennoble as 'constancy', and the next call 'will to get her own way'); an accomplished opportunism or a good head for scheming; and the purely pragmatic virtue of success in action. The sum total of this as 'virtue' is not ethically satisfying.

Rossiter here goes from a refusal to deal with the moral question he poses, is Helena 'Virtue itself?' – not it seems to me the kind of question on the agenda of this or any other play by Shakespeare –, to a refusal to deal with the psychological question, is Helena a single, consistent quality? After defining the 'two particles in this mysterious, alleged unity', Rossiter observes that this quality of Helena produces 'mixed feelings in which the fairy-tale solution we might like to believe in . . . is in conflict with the realistic, psychological exposure – which is very much more convincing'.

Some of the difficulties Rossiter faced in his lecture on *All's Well* arose from the weight of Romantic criticism, which had moralised Helena into a paragon, and of folkloristic criticism, which had given the illusion of substance to this view by insisting it was a law of folk-tale that Clever Wenches were necessarily Right in all things. If Rossiter did not question the relevance of imposing moral abstractions on Helena in the first place, or the implications of a longing for fairy-tale solutions, he made clear the intended pervasiveness and theatrical force of the ironies and contradictions critics had wished away or condemned as blunders. Rossiter's warning us off attempts to analyse Helena as roads to confusion seems curious now in light of the clarity of his summary. His final sentence, however, may explain a great deal: 'The sum total of this as "virtue" is not ethically satisfying.' The difficulties may lie in the eyes of message-hunting beholders rather than in the character of Helena, in their expectations and desires for 'moral' meanings. Perhaps even if we leave moral expectations in abeyance, Helena will remain a kind of conundrum, yet even conundrums have shapes and differ from one another, and they can certainly teach us something of their social context and of the technical problems Shakespeare faced in creating his protagonist.

Yet perhaps the difficulties lay as much in the author as in the task. Does the Helena who, like Browning's Guido, 'determined, dared, and did/The deed just as [s]he purposed, point to point', represent the poet's admiration of the free-standing woman, much like his admiration of the Dark Lady? And does the other Helena, the Helena of meek anguish and self-accusation, represent a counter-

thought, Shakespeare's reservations about a woman's
triumph at the expense of sexual and class conventions,
again reminiscent of his reservations about the Dark Lady?
The poor physician's daughter has managed to bestow,
not *lose*, her virginity, and *not* to a man's liking, but
entirely to her own, reducing the man to an unwitting
instrument, and climbing from servant to Countess in the
bargain. Helena's question to Parolles about losing her
virginity to her own liking was a revolutionary manifesto
in the interrogative, and no less so for its having always
been asked by women if only silently. Susan Snyder, who
has written on Helena's shifts from assertiveness to self-
abnegation, wonders whether some of her anomalies of
character are due to Shakespeare's uneasiness at her
violation of the rules of patriarchy. Snyder sees the
invocation of providence as an attempt to mask or mitigate
the subversiveness of Helena's triumphant initiative. The
argument is persuasive. But should one attribute the
contradictions in Helena specifically to Shakespeare's
uneasiness? A. P. Rossiter has argued for the ambivalence
of the history plays, their narrative patterns accommodating now a providential idea of history, now history as the
product of secular will. Helena's self-doubts and her
continuing initiative are paralleled by, say, Henry V's,
although for Henry there is of course no gesture of
withdrawal, even one as questionable as Helena's. At
times it is useful to query the generic distinctions and see
the Problem Plays as only extreme instances of their
author's settled practice. Shakespeare's mature plays set
out action and thought as referable to both providential
schemes and human cause; such was the problematic early
seventeenth-century interpretative agenda. But complex
narrative from Homer on employs multiple causation
implying both a pattern of determinism whatever its cast
– religious or secular – and a pattern of voluntarism whose
particular character is also coloured by the historical
moment. One wonders whether Shakespeare contrived
character and event for the sake of conveying the patterns

or accepted the patterns for the sake of complexity in character and event.

If we cannot be certain of Shakespeare's uneasiness about violations of patriarchy, we can be certain that his audiences came to the plays with divided views. But just how uneasy would Helena's success have made even the most backward thinking? Here Snyder's point is telling: Helena's meekness and self-doubt are useful concessions to sexist attitudes, as is also the play's evocation of providence. But equally important is *All's Well*'s inescapable fairy-tale plot. Finally, Helena is a woman, and the famous weddings of princes to kitchen-maids and kings to nubile beggars, far from being revolutionary, validate patriarchy. Had the upstart been a male Helenus, touchy audiences would surely have been offended.

A thoroughly conventional Helena would never have engaged any man in solitary conversation, let alone a Parolles, and especially in a discussion of virginity. What convention dictated as proper was elaborated endlessly in sermons and books on female conduct, instilled in the household circle and maintained through the sort of oversight and calling to account that Helena undergoes in the first act. As a kind of ward of the Countess, Helena was treated like an aristocratic daughter and had to conform to standards beyond those to which a waiting-gentlewoman might have been held even in a household as well ordered as the Countess of Rossillion's. The powerful interview between the Countess and Helena is not only a trial of whether Helena has gone beyond what is proper to her rank but, more generally, whether she has gone beyond the bounds of female modesty. Part of the vitality of the exchange between the two women comes from its being overdetermined. The Countess's questions and Helena's replies are shaped not only by the pressures of status but by the pressure of what is expected of women and beyond this by the debts and intimacies of their particular situation. The dialogue's multiplicity of reference imparts an impression of wavering implication

and multiple cause like that of significant, actual talk.
Helena acquits herself well. Her responses are models of
embarrassed reticence and deferential respect. When at
last she is forced to admit her love for Bertram, she insists
that it is 'honest', free from evil intention and proper in
its expression, that is in its remaining unexpressed. In
her lengthy speech of confession (I.iii.186–212), Helena
reiterates her modest passivity ('I follow him not/By any
token of presumptuous suit'), and her resignation to the
likelihood that her love is hopeless and will remain 'riddle-
like' (unknown), and that she will live 'sweetly [i.e.
silently] where she dies'. The last line presents almost too
pretty and conventional a picture of contented self-
sacrifice. At any rate it prompts a sharp question from
the Countess about Helena's proposed journey to Paris.
Well it might, for despite Helena's despairing metaphors
for the futility of her love – pouring waters into a sieve,
adoring the sun – what Helena has described is not the
easily dismissed infatuation of immaturity. And she has
spoken one line, 'Nor would I have him till I do deserve
him', that opens the glimmer of a possibility, despite
Helena's immediate denial that she can conceive of how
to actually come to deserve Bertram. It is going too far
to accuse Helena of trying to deceive the Countess here.
What she says is literally true. She has never approached
Bertram with her love nor does she intend to; the
overwhelming likelihood *is* that nothing will come of it.
The offer to cure the King is so piously problematic a
way of 'deserving' Bertram that even the Countess can
accept it as an innocent means to that end. In going to
Paris, Helena proposes only to try her luck and her 'stars';
curing the King is a worthy end in itself, a proper act of
womanly service.

If Helena is not deceiving the Countess, she is not
deceiving herself either. Her father's 'good receipt/Shall
for [her] legacy be sanctified/By the luckiest stars in
heaven . . .'. In short, if she succeeds, her father's cure
will become her dowry, a dowry enhanced by a particular

blessing. So favoured, she will await what may follow. As much of a plot to gain Bertram as there is in this, Helena is willing to state and the Countess ready to accept. The scene is remarkably adroit in preserving both the Countess's and Helena's 'modesty' and respect for station even as it furthers Helena's necessarily daring activism. Only at the beginning of Act 3 Scene 2 does the Countess say, 'It hath happened all as I would have had it, save that he comes not along with her.'

Helena's modesty is even more precariously balanced in her appeal to the Countess's own experience as she attempts to reconcile the intensity of her love with a due regard for womanly propriety. Helena's description of her feeling takes the form of a question whether the Countess, in 'so true a flame of liking', did ever 'wish [so] chastely and love [so] dearly, that your Dian/Was both herself and love?' Had the Countess in her youth ever felt at once her own innocence *and* sexual desire? If so she should pity Helena. This goes further than either hypocrisy or canny prudence would have gone. It is not only confession but a plea for absolution. Quite properly the Countess ignores it as rather too personal, even given her feelings for Helena.

Yet we already have the answer. The Countess's brief soliloquy just before Helena enters has told us. This nine-line reflection on young love (I.iii.123–32), her own and Helena's, is as intellectually rich as it is moving, and in its brevity presents the emotion both recollected and re-experienced. Among other things, love – which the Countess does not doubt Helena is feeling, if only because of her own observations – confirms the link of women to nature and signals their proper maturation even as it makes youth painful. In the recollecting, young love seems a fault, in the experiencing, none; yet to observe it is to observe an illness. The Countess's reflections are free of moralism and self-concern, at once sympathetic, disinterested and full of the attractiveness of the speaker. Love here is a 'Life Force', but rather less bleakly glandular than Shaw's, more in the nature of a garden growth, as much to be cultivated and as pleasurable, despite the dangers; hardly the impersonal power that entraps Shaw's Jack Tanner, in whose case love is made to seem almost beside the point. The acceptance and irony of the later Sonnets are here wreathed in intense sympathy and, as there, we are given not a word of procreation or of transcendence.

There is obviously a disparity between the character and intensity of the feelings invoked by the two women and Helena's actual relations with Bertram. Are those feelings the delusion of women's youth and the sentimentalism of their old age, and so yet another of *All's Well's* mordant ironies? The King's recollection of Bertram's father can persuade us that at least in the case of the Countess such emotions may have found a proper object and reciprocity. For Helena such consummations, already made doubtful by what we have seen of Bertram, become more remote as the play unfolds.

The contrast between the idealising warmth of Helena's feeling for Bertram and the actuality of their relations is obviously intended. It suggests the commonplace gap between what was thought and advised about love and marriage and the uncorresponding actualities of contemporary life which are transformed in the play. Historical knowledge allows one to be more certain about relevant laws and rituals, somewhat less certain about what was thought and advised (at least out of print), and less certain still about the representativeness of particular domestic arrangements for which we have some evidence. One should take as suggestive rather than definitive Lawrence Stone's assertion in *The Family, Sex and Marriage in England 1500–1800* (p. 644) that 'the late sixteenth and early seventeenth centuries was the only period in history when the three basic motives for marriage [love, desire and procreation] were more or less united in the thinking of theologians and moralists'. Some evidence for Stone's assertion is to be found in the most public of documents. The Homily on Marriage, the eighteenth among many read on Sundays in Anglican churches after 1562, admonished, '. . . ye wives be in subjugation to obey your husbands . . . for he is the head of the woman, as Christ is the head of the Church.' At the same time, however, even religious moralists preached mutuality, if not equality, in sermons based on St Jerome's observation that Eve had been made not from Adam's head or from his foot, but from Adam's side, that she might 'walk joyntly with him, under the conduct and government of her head'. The possessive pronoun here says much. The third element, desire, was an even trickier matter for sermons. Yet here again the example of Eve was preached on. She was evidence of the greater sexual appetite and frailty of heart of woman, who, the Homily declared, 'is a weak creature not endued with like [i.e. man's] strength and constancy of mind'. Again with the Fall in mind sermons declared that 'nothing is more impure than to love a wife like an adulterous woman'. For all this, the striking interchange of religious and erotic imagery in the poetry of John Donne will seem less private and extreme if one recalls the phrasing of the marriage ceremony: 'and with my body I thee worship'. Its implications leave the status of desire problematic. As the century wore on, however, the possibility of sexuality as a natural pleasure gave way to the view that it was only a mark of fallen mankind.

Marriage in the early decades of the seventeenth century, however, was affected, as were all aspects of public and private life, by the loosening of old bonds and customs. Romantic love as an ideal or as a desirable state of natural pleasure was given currency by the arts; inevitably romantic art assumed and depicted an elevated status for women as rationally desirable and actually desired. Further, the Puritan tendency to moralise social commitments led to the conception of 'Holy Matrimony', a state in which love was joined to procreation. Instead of a contractual arrangement to preserve property and power, marriage was proposed as a blessed alliance for, among other goals, companionship and comfort. Depending as it did on mutual respect and honesty, Holy Matrimony tended to elevate woman's status and call into question the double standard. It can be argued, however, that in some marriages romantic ideals of love only bound women more completely to routine and self-sacrifice.

Lafew's offer of his daughter, apparently perfunctory and weakly rationalised by Bertram only after the fact, seems hardly unusual in this context, either in its obvious political and economic aspects or in Bertram's insistence that 'At first/I stuck my choice upon' Maudlin. It reflects the early seventeenth-century character of upper-class marriages which attempted to satisfy the claims of interest while nodding at the newer values of marital harmony. Lafew's suggestion that Bertram 'give a favour from you/ To sparkle' in Maudlin's spirits 'That she may quickly come' is dreadfully uncomprehending of the newer style represented by Bertram's rationalisation – hollow though both gestures are.

Despite changes in the conception of marriage, many young women in the highest ranks of society, save for their obviously easier material conditions, were worse off than their social inferiors. Often enough, as Keith Wrightson points out in chapter four of *English Society 1580–1680* (1982), they could be merely 'ornamental and idle', filling up solitary lives with needlework while their husbands were off on private and public business. They could grow to regret, as did Ann Clifford, the 'marble pillars' of their manorial grandeur as 'but the gay arbours of anguish'. Such gilded alienation was in part the result of marriages which were frankly economic and caste arrangements rather than unions of personal choice. In part, however, it arose from a feeling of uselessness, of having little role to play beyond social self-display and the regular production of legitimate heirs. Although her diary (1599–1605) tells us that Lady Margaret Hoby often discussed business affairs with Sir Thomas, this was apparently unusual, and wives of her class could not typically immerse themselves in the dawn-to-dark *doing* that constituted the daily round and gave variety, purpose and a sense of self-worth to the lives of 'less fortunate' women. Whatever economy it effected, Shakespeare's removal of Giletta's period as chatelaine from his story has the historically suggestive result of increasing Helena's dependency on the relation with Bertram.

One result of their placement largely outside the worlds of work and responsibility was the trivialisation of the lives of aristocratic women, their extreme dependency on husbands through whose activities they attempted to live vicariously. Given the injunctions of the Homilies and the realities of their lives, it is not surprising that the letters and diaries of gentlewomen often agree in spirit with Lady Mildmay's Helena-like reflections after the death of her husband: 'I carried alwayes that reverent respect towards him . . . that I could not fynde it in my heart to challenge him for the worst word or deede which ever he offered me . . .'.

What must have made their situation even more difficult was the greater opportunity for aristocratic young women to envisage alternatives to the kind of marriage most of them were to have. They had greatest access to the promises of the arts and the fantasies of leisure. Romantic love, Lawrence Stone tells us, existed in the households of princes and great nobles. Gascoigne's *Adventures of Master F. J.* and Wyatt's lyrics are suggestive of the ambience. Moreover, the Court was a social setting almost uniquely suited to casual acquaintance among the marriageable young, a place far different from the supervised isolation and limited entertainments of many country seats. The curiously elliptical opening of Helena's speech beginning at I.i.160, partly addressed to Parolles, mostly a reverie, states precisely her fears about Bertram's going to the Court: 'There shall your master have a thousand loves . . . The court's a learning place . . .'. Her fears of court attractions and the variety of women there, rather than any self-aggrandising account of her own infinite variety (out of character for Helena in any case), seem the burdens of this puzzling speech.

For many of the well-born of both sexes, however, the Court was a learning place whose lessons of free choice, mutuality and ideal love (lessons, it is true, offered along with the quite different ones that Philip Sidney and Bertram learned) were never to be applied. Their situations were to be much like Bertram's: a world opened for them, and as suddenly closed.

Brutally put, the élite young, especially young women, were less free in the choice of life-partners than were their inferiors: their marriages were largely marriages of convenience – the economic and social convenience of others. Lawrence Stone writes: 'Only if a girl of aristocratic family possessed enormous persistence, obstinacy and strength of will could she hope to marry the individual of her choice.' Lacking Helena's lucky cure, Mary, the daughter of the Earl of Cork, triumphed because of her fanatical religious piety. Stone may be exaggerating the difficulties in the way of love matches, but many difficulties there were.

The reason for society's trying to keep tight control over aristocratic marriages and over women both before and after marriage was bluntly stated well over a century later by Dr Johnson: 'All the property of the world depends on female chastity.' The greater the property the greater the impulse to control. From this central consideration was elaborated a multitude of legal and behavioural constraints, some of them apparently so remote from the requirements of primogeniture as to have lost sight of it. Marriage, in the words of Defoe's Roxana, at the far end of the century and after feminist claims had been more loudly voiced, was 'nothing but giving up liberty, estate, authority, and everything . . . [becoming] a mere woman ever after – that is to say a slave'. Though widowhood might offer some – as it did the Countess of Rossillion – a measure of freedom *after* marriage, even she had still the disabilities imposed by Bertram's required wardship. And *before* marriage, women were also women, equally if not more subject to male control, disabling laws and conventions of conduct.

In *The Whole Duty of a Woman* (1985), Angeline Goreau's anthology of seventeenth-century writing by women, just what such conventionality entailed is clearly laid out. It was essentially a bleak discipline of thought and behaviour indicative of sexual constraint. Women's 'honour' – virginity before marriage and fidelity afterwards – testified to the control of fathers, and then of husbands, and finally to the legitimate inheritance of control by sons. From p(r)udence were elaborated codes of speech, dress, gesture, feeling, vocation and routine; and beyond them the higher feminine virtues of obedience, piety, self-sacrifice and silence. Shakespeare's elaborate play with the voices of women and their silence (in Cordelia and Virgilia, for instance) is testimony to a particular social alertness. Fortunately, actualities are less rigid than codes. Humane affection, romantic love and the emerging ideals of individual liberty mitigated the personal situations of many wives and daughters. But for all the common sense of women as against male folly in *Love's Labour's Lost*, for example, for all the implied promise that the Rosalind of *As You like It* and the Beatrice of *Much Ado* can be sharers rather than mere subjects in marriage, the best that their spectator-sisters might hope for was a flexible, even a loving, mutuality but only *within* the rules; and a mutuality that demanded not only their observance but, when required, the display of that observance; in short, the ambiguous felicity of Katherine at the end of *The Taming of the Shrew*. Contemporary criticism and performance have perhaps made too much of a mystery of *The Taming of the Shrew* in an effort to mitigate the defence of female subservience in Kate's culminating fifth-act speech on marriage. But its import cannot be wholly acted or interpreted away. If irony or gaiety or eccentricity or sweet collusion are brought forth to transform, no, elucidate the text, it is because they are obviously needed. The alternative to nullity, distance or a Kate-like happiness was the 'upside-down' dominance of the shrew; not, at least for comedy, an attractive ending, although John Fletcher was to use the idea in a later play. The law, the counsels of received opinion and the circumstances of aristocratic marriage were designed to induce the kind of reverent adulation and patience recorded in the earlier excerpt from Lady Mildmay's Diary. However it is interpreted, *The Taming of the Shrew* suggests how problematic that state of patience and submission could be. It is not only the whole of Helena's career that calls that submissiveness into question; as in *The Taming of the Shrew* it is the possibilities of the ending. The elaborate devices that lead to the unmasking of Bertram, with their rings, fables and witnesses, have an absorbing staginess which Shakespeare apparently liked well enough as dramaturgy to use in the last act of *Measure for Measure*. But it is a terrible machine that teases Bertram along and then traps him painfully in lie after lie. Giletta's holiday return allows Beltramo a gracious celebration in which to distance and right his error. But Helena pretty well destroys Bertram, who wraps himself in whatever wisp of self-respect is offered by the rhetoric of a conditional sentence.

Almost from the beginning, *All's Well* suggests the problematic nature of submissiveness, if not the Countess's then Helena's. Putting aside her great aim to marry Bertram, Helena's behaviour as spinster and spouse looks unimpeachably conventional – almost. Her first soliloquy shows her resolved to worship Bertram from afar; her second, not to pursue Bertram, but to deserve him. She reaffirms these marks of propriety in her interview with the Countess. When the King at first refuses to allow her to attempt the cure, Helena declares that she 'will no more enforce mine office'. When he continues his excuses, she intelligently senses a half-hidden willingness, and returns to the argument, using the same appeal to providence she had used in justifying her motives for the trip to Paris. It is perhaps the only argument reasonably consistent with female propriety. She argues it would be presumption in the King (as in herself) to attribute a cure that is the work of heaven to the skill of a mere agent. When in the husband-choosing scene she comes at last to face Bertram, she is eloquently conventional in saying that she does not take him, but rather gives herself in lifelong service. When Bertram objects she retreats, saying to the King, 'That you are well restored, my lord, I'm glad. Let the rest go.' In this as in earlier instances, Helena seems to pull away from the determined Giletta of the Boccaccian plot, which, however, has the King shortly overrule her reticences and demurrers. After the marriage, she listens unquestioningly to Parolles' presentation of Bertram's commands, replying only, 'In everything I wait upon his will.' All this culminates in Act 2 Scene 5, when Bertram refuses to hear her apologetic resolution to make up for her lowly birth 'With true observance'; 'dutiful service and reverence' is the usual gloss of this phrase. When she speaks of timorously desiring to steal what the law now allows her, she accepts Bertram's refusal by stating her own refusal to name her desire (a kiss), and does so with only an oblique reference. She ends with, 'I shall not break your bidding, my good lord.' Even after she has unmasked Bertram and revealed her identity, she asks Bertram 'Will you be mine?' Until she has male approval, she is 'but the shadow of a wife'. Such is the submissive Helena.

Shakespeare is rarely the prisoner of his materials. Yet retaining Boccaccio's story while rethinking its values imposed severe restrictions on the task of characterising Helena. Boccaccio's Clever Wench had only to be given the particular social skills and style appropriate to the upper-class setting to fall in perfectly with the folk-tale. But Shakespeare was, on the face of it, not content to make a comedy of a predatory heroine or even of one merely dogged and successful. The French actor, Louis

Jouvet, once remarked, 'Success justifies everything and explains nothing.' If he was not a dogmatist, Shakespeare was certainly a fine explainer since the theatre's demand for probabilities is implicitly a demand for explanations. Helena could not be simply an inexplicable success, one merely dictated by the genre. She was to have the virtue and complexity, and exhibit the friction between role and disposition, that make his other leading women worth caring about. For Shakespeare comedy required not only feasts and marriages but a fortunate deserving.

In part the resulting difficulty with *All's Well* came from the imposition of a Griselda upon a Giletta, submissiveness on activism, silence on daring. As Giletta perfectly fits her story, Griselda is perfectly accommodated to hers. It is not Griselda who chooses her noble husband; she is elevated (and discharged, and elevated once again) at the will of others. The career of Helena interrupts Griselda with Giletta; the result tempts partial or cynical interpretations. As we have seen, Shakespeare takes several measures to reconcile Helena's apparent extremes, among them Helena's apologies and self-justification at crucial points in the play, and – connected with this – a questioning inwardness. This self-questioning, like that of Hamlet, offers the reassurance of moral scruple if not the certainty of self-knowledge and right action. By such devices he attempts to sustain the illusion of a continued conformity to the conventions of womanly submissiveness by a woman whose love has sent her on an obviously unconventional course of action. Helena's particular social circumstances require this conventionality. In loving Orlando in *As You Like It* Rosalind will marry down, an unconventional act allowable by reason of the liberatingly *déclassé* conditions of exile and the democratising force of the forest of Arden. Helena, however, is nothing but a serving gentlewoman and must act more 'nobly' than the nobility. Yet her heartfelt soliloquy at the end of Act 3 Scene 2, vividly envisioning Bertram's dangers in war, and ending with the guilty decision to leave Rossillion so

Bertram can return safely, is Shakespeare's effort to elicit our sympathy for Helena and clear her of the accusation of being only a schemer. That her motive here is almost immediately clouded by the dubious pilgrimage and its hardly happenstance objective, Florence, is a reminder of the intractable thematic implications of the story. Its succession of incidents implies motives which Helena's self-questioning, apologies and reflections overlap but do not erase. Intellectual confusion and artistic failure are two judgements on the result. Yet these do not exhaust the possibilities.

The Griselda and Giletta stories have one thing in common: they are too good to be true; perhaps this is the nature of exemplary tales. The survival, let alone the triumph of perfect female submission – and the survival, let alone the triumph, of love and desire in the face of total rejection – are exemplary male fables of gender. Both assume the disposable nature of woman's self-respect and the absolute, self-evident attractiveness of the male. In both cases – total passive submissiveness and total active dedication – the reward of 'success' is the male's ultimate acceptance of the heroine because she has demonstrated that she is literally self-less. Telescoping the two paradigmatic tales of Griselda and Giletta allows each to call the other in question by suggesting the unrealities of the alternative position. This paradoxical result of combining the two archetypal conduct-tales is most concentrated in the bed-trick, where activity and passivity join to create an event at once highly manipulative and highly self-destructive. Helena is both obedient and treacherous to Bertram, self-serving and self-denying, deeply insulted and doubly gratified. But perhaps this is to over-intellectualise Shakespeare's narrative strategy, although the paradoxes and ironies of *All's Well* and the speculative concern with abstract ideas which *All's Well* shares with the other Problem Comedies certainly give us warrant to step back from the text for a moment and view it as at a distance. In any case, if the ironies of Helena's responses and of her course of submissiveness and daring point to ideas, they also point to everyday realities.

Noel Annan's revised biography of Virginia Woolf's father, the journalist and man of letters Leslie Stephen, has several passages descriptive of Stephen's views on women, their education, their mental capacities and destined role which would not have been out of place in a seventeenth-century gentleman's commonplace book. It is all there, the notions of the limitations of the female mind, the strictures against a university education, the certainty that women's only proper vocation is that of helpmate and sustainer. Readers of Woolf's *To the Lighthouse* or of her essays will not be shocked by her father's opinions, though there was more – and better – to Leslie Stephen than this. However, they may well wonder at the extent to which Stephen's second wife, Woolf's mother, Julia – a woman of wide sympathy and intellectual power and generally 'advanced' opinions – concurred in her husband's views. Stephen's demand for devotion was draining, and Woolf was to speculate that had he not died, she would have died intellectually. She was later to write something of the sort – metaphorically – about her mother. The motives and contexts of Elizabethan and Victorian patriarchy were different, but some of their internal dynamics were the same. Willing acceptance by women, as Stone observes (*Family and Marriage*, p. 151), was the key to the survival of the Elizabethan system of patriarchy in marriage. Willing acceptance is also a key to survival *within* such systems. It can transform burdens and impositions into psychological needs. The demands placed on the conduct of women amounted to a female code of honour, at once a burden, an incentive and a source of pride much cherished by all the women in the play, spoken for eloquently by Mariana, Diana and the Widow, and acted out by Helena.

Male honour depended on physical courage, easily tested, and on the reliability of one's word, again testable. But woman's honour depended on reputation and reputation depended on the least word of everyone from prince to milkmaid. It is possible to go through a lifetime without having to discover one's cowardice – easier now than then perhaps – or being discovered in a lie. But women's least actions were subject to opinion. Hence the pathological wariness of those exemplary Elizabethan women who even in widowed old age admitted no male visitor save by day – with doors open and servants present.

Through later instances and Renaissance documents we can realise now something of the texture of relations that wavered, as does the relation of Petruchio and Kate in *The Taming of the Shrew*, from oppression to compliance to consent to participation and mutuality. Rewards there surely were, certainly the ineradicable if intermittent ones of love and parenthood, and the conventional rewards of fidelity to customary and approved models. But the texture of experience must have been different, familiar as certain types, like the manipulative-conformist Bianca of *The Taming of the Shrew*, may seem. Even Katherine Mansfield might have allowed that scheming and 'cleverness' become different – less reprehensible and probably less lethal weapons – in contexts of settled and accepted domination. But still there were means other than 'strategy'. For Helena, however, direct confrontation was not one of them. Her cause was love, not justice; her social station also limited her means. In being at once submissive and spirited, Helena seems at least as much of her day as the heroines of Shakespeare's sunnier comedies of love. Examples of firmness within submissiveness, self-assertion within the rules of a game that denied it, suggest that Helena had counterparts. Keith Wrightson (p. 95) cites the example of Ann Clifford, who had the spirit to resist not only her husband, the Duke of Dorset, but King James himself over the question of giving up her claim to her father's lands, yet accepted meekly the unkind treatment meted out to her for her resistance. A whole range of sentiments and responses – however contradictory or covert – clustering around the maintenance of integrity must have found vent even in those marriages at the most oppressive end of the spectrum. To understand their strategy we should perhaps look not only to examples from contemporary and even Victorian marriages but also recall the psychology of the Sonnets with their often ironic blend of abject love, guarded confrontation and poetic self-assertiveness. It is tempting to think: as the Poet of the Sonnets, so Helena; each is trapped in an intense yet empty love distorted by what are essentially differences of status, doubly distorted in the case of Helena, who is not only a poor physician's daughter but a woman, that is, doubly a member of a lower class. In any case, acceptance of the unfair rules of the game did not preclude either reward or resistance; it transformed them.

Something of the process by which the supposed disabilities of women – disdained by men – were turned into rewards are revealed at several points in the play. When the Countess praises Helena for honesty and goodness, for gifts which her virtue will properly employ, Lafew observes that 'Your commendations, madam, get from her tears'. To this the Countess replies, "Tis the best brine a maiden can season her praise in.' Why was Helena in tears? The Countess's next sentence suggests that Helena was crying because of the mention of her dead father. Helena's next speech, cryptic but later explained in her soliloquy, hints that it is the departure of Bertram that sets her crying, possibly, if we use the hindsight of the soliloquy, with some measure of guilt that longing for Bertram has pre-empted an obligatory mourning for her father. But even if she is not weeping over her praise, as the sequence of topics suggests, the Countess's first comment puts in an aphorism the psychological deformations expected of women. Their praise was to be preserved and made palatable (seasoned) by sorrow; logically, then, the praise of women required something to be made acceptable, and their sorrow was expected to be liberal, coming either from their fate as women (though the implications of this were not pursued), or from their immediate sense of their sex's unworthiness for praise. Virtues (womanly virtues at least) were made of this endless tangle of repressions, underestimations and guilts that turned even the celebration of gifts into an occasion for tears – in part marks of self-denial – and the tears themselves into a proof of appropriate womanly behaviour. What a delicious irony that Parolles, no doubt as great 'a whale to virginity' (could he only swim) as his master Bertram, should be the occasion of Helena's liberation from the cycle of virginal passivity!

The argument Parolles uses, unwittingly, to free Helena is the argument Bertram later uses to seduce Diana. Both declare the virgin a traitor to her mother, and in doing so accuse virginity of unnaturalness, of wanting passion, being 'cold and stern', a 'withered pear'. Given the Elizabethan 'settlement' between the sexes, these are precisely the most telling arguments. They speak to woman's inculcated role as the guardian and repository of emotion, and as 'close to nature' and the source of new generations. The irony that it is this very emotionality and supposed bondage to nature that are occasions for male disdain should not be lost. Helena is not taken in by Parolles, but rather reminded that by temperament and passion (for Bertram) and by her desire for the full role of woman, she is not to be such a virgin as Parolles sketches. There is desire (liking) in Helena; on stage she is a sensual presence, if properly acted, but in her, pleasure is not separated from procreation as it is in Bertram, if he ever thinks of the latter. Bertram's impossible commands to Helena are just the two she has already undertaken: the sharing of his family honour and the bearing of his children.

Shakespeare intended Helena to be played as at least charming and physically attractive, perhaps even unusually so, and no doubt the adolescent male actors could convey this impression. For Boccaccio's Beltramo Shakespeare gives us a Bertram, but for other characters he invents significant names: Parolles, Lavatch, Lafew, Diana, the brothers Dumain. He does not translate Giletta as Jill or Gillian. Both English cognates have even more of the open field and milking-stool about them than does Lavatch's Isbel, hardly the effect Shakespeare wanted. In transforming Giletta into Helena he provided the other extreme, a figure with legendary associations of a beauty that launched a thousand ships. Something like beauty Helena surely has, if we are to believe Lafew's indignant enthusiasm for her during the husband-choosing scene, his earlier arch epithet for her as 'pretty lady' and for himself as Cressid's uncle, and the King's judgement of her as not only wise but fair. Several times she is spoken of as 'sweet'. But this Helen launches only one military unit – Bertram, and her own expeditions to Paris and to Florence are the most impressive campaigns of the play. If she is not quite a Helen in beauty and desirability, however, she herself is sensuous and passionate.

The intellectuality of the play and the complexities of Helena herself keep us at a reasoning distance from the chief character. Yet the warmth of Helena's feeling, her desire as well as her desirability, are strongly conveyed in the soliloquies, the interview with the Countess and the husband-choosing scene. Her frank discussion of her feelings in the scene with Parolles, however, has seemed to some 'out of character' or at worst evidence of duplicity rather than dualism. How is it possible that this 'proper symbol of virtue' can speak to the likes of Parolles so openly of losing her virginity? There are two different questions here. The first, a moral question, simply disappears if one rejects the notions of Helena as symbol, and of virginity as in itself a sign of moral superiority for Shakespeare. Although the arguments against virginity come out of the mouths of Parolles and Bertram and are in both instances applied in mean causes, the arguments from the need to perpetuate the race and to enjoy the sensuous fullness of life are arguments with which the dramatist evidently agreed. In his plays the ascetic idea is laughed at before and after *Love's Labour's Lost*. Parolles' final words of advice to Helena have been taken as both proper and enlightened. 'Get thee a good husband, and use him as he uses thee. So, farewell.' Some interpret this as an 'advanced' advocacy of mutuality in marriage. But this is to mis-equate tit for tat with sharing. Parolles' first clause is apt enough, but his second smacks of the vulgarly pragmatic or the cynical; however, he seems to predict the course of Helena's future behaviour. Everything depends on getting 'a *good* husband' and so Parolles on wifely behaviour is hardly advice for all seasons. But this much more should be said for Parolles: he apparently recognises the right of a wife to return blow for blow. There seems to be in him something of the instinctive solidarity of the underdog.

The interview with Parolles is a scene that had to be written. How and why Helena – or indeed anyone – falls in love is best dispersed in hints and largely assumed at the outset of a play. It may also occur between acts, but how and why a principal moves from resignation to heroic action is matter for showing rather than telling. Moreover, to establish exactly the sort of love that is Helena's motive is to establish her good faith, something required by her inferior circumstances. Parolles is perhaps the one character in the play to whom she can speak with few cautions about some aspects of her predicament. There are obvious barriers with the Countess. But from the first she has a kind of conspiratorial understanding with Parolles. The relation must be carefully defined. To the Countess Helena can communicate the object and the intensity of her feelings, but she will get no reply to her query about sexuality – about being *both* Diana *and* love. To Parolles she can communicate nothing of the object and intensity of her feelings, but she can raise certain social questions to which the Countess cannot respond. Helena hardly trusts Parolles or his advice. Her brief 'character' of him just before Parolles enters in the first scene is often quoted, one of the striking bits of acute observation in the play's ironic mode. For Bertram's sake she loves this liar, fool and coward, recognising in him a kind of perfection of the type that enables him to 'take place', i.e. take precedence, over virtue, which can appear most unattractive at times. The speech has inappropriately been taken as a piece of Helena's unpleasant serpent-wisdom rather than as a piece of her realism or as an example of her simply human delight in the droll, which is shared later by the soldiers, even at the height of Parolles' insulting betrayals of them, and by Lafew, who spots Parolles as a scoundrel at once. Helena, in short, recognises Parolles as an eminently social creature, who, if not worldly-wise, is worldly-canny, just such a one as can give her the (male) world's view of reluctant virginity reluctant to be undone.

Their dialogue is far less serious than the questions it addresses, and it begins with a fine and revealing *jeu d'esprit*.

> *Parolles* Save you, fair queen!
> *Helena*   And you, monarch!
> *Parolles* No.
> *Helena*   And no.

(I.i.104–70)

This cryptic exchange establishes the basis of their shallow and tenuous complicity. Both have managed to attain circumstances above their social lot, Helena through merit and the Countess's grace and favour, Parolles through a quite different sort of merit and to some extent the grace and favour of Bertram. Parolles' greeting to Helena as queen makes ironic light of this social elevation. She takes the point and replies in kind. From there on little touches of speech continue the ironic mutual condescension of those who know each other's story. For Helena Parolles has in him 'some stain of soldier'. For Parolles Helena is one to be hectored with voluble exhortation: 'Away with't!' and 'Keep it not' – virginity being the antecedent of the pronoun – and, with, 'Little Helen, farewell. If I can remember thee I will think of thee at court.' But this last, a less pleasant kind of condescension, comes after Helena's avoidance of his pointedly inviting question about her virginity: 'Will you anything with it?' Helena pays attention to Parolles' arguments, but not to Parolles, and her reflections on the Court convey a sexual warmth clearly not meant for him. She responds to Parolles with a smart repartee on his cowardice, so effective that he has to withdraw lamely from the contest of wits: 'I am so full of businesses I cannot answer thee accurately.' But he pursues his immodest proposal in a promise to return 'perfect courtier', when he will '*understand* what advice shall *thrust*' upon her or '*die* in her unthankfulness'. (The *double entendres* are italicised.) Helena pays no attention: she has understood Parolles on virginity, but will apply the lesson to his master.

Helena is not the only one of Shakespeare's leading women to be both Diana *and* Love, both chaste and erotically intense, or the only one of such women to trade witticisms with a scoundrel – in the case of Desdemona, with something worse than a scoundrel. The combination of passion and propriety, of activism and submissiveness, can take a tragic direction, as it does in *Othello*, where Desdemona is, in a very different context, also the active suitor, prompting Othello's declaration of love and his proposal of marriage. Her urging of Cassio's cause is not ambitious meddling but the working of the sometimes naïve sense of justice that led her to defy Venice and love Othello in the first place. Her awful submissiveness toward the end of the play is wholly compatible with it. But it is also Desdemona who openly demands that the Venetian Senate allow her to accompany Othello to Cyprus, since she '[did] love the Moor to live with him', and would not give up 'The rites for why I love him . . .'. It is the same Desdemona, too, who encourages the all-too-willing Iago to speak what she calls 'fond paradoxes to make fools laugh in the alehouse', off-colour slanders of women's chastity. Yet she seems to enjoy them well enough. Despite her mock-condemnation, they have a use: 'I am not merry, but I do beguile/The thing I am [i.e. sad] by seeming otherwise.' Some of what criticism has found contradictory in Helena, the jostle of innocence with sexual passion, of submissiveness with aggressive action, and of all these with what seems like an appreciative ear (and tongue) for witty smut can be found elsewhere in Shakespeare's heroines. What seems contradictory follows from both 'unrealistic' dramaturgy and from a 'realistic' conception of women. Sometimes Shakespeare's characters tell the audience what he thinks they need to know or will be moved by, even if doing so entails their stepping out of stage character. Soliloquies are unrealistic, as is such language in adolescents as Juliet's expression of fear that Death not Romeo might steal her maidenhead. But in both cases the content can be thought of as realistically conceived by the poet, revealing a clash of motifs in human thought and feeling that need to be seen as 'unified' only in the monoliths of critical commentary or narrow moralism.

To Stone's triad of motives for marriage, love, desire and procreation, we should add a fourth, Boccaccio's 'honest comfort', already part of the idea of Holy Matrimony. Elizabethan theology did not make a harmony of the four, though some happy marriages may have. But typically, before, after and during marriage, one guesses that the four largely remained side by side, discrete, unassimilated in any Platonic transcendence, none quite reducible to any of the others. So it is in *All's Well* and elsewhere in Shakespeare, most notably in *Measure for Measure*. Both are plays in which Shakespeare's departure from the patterns of comic and tragic genres, and the implications of the particular plots he chose, result in a heavy emphasis on the commonplace disparateness of human motive and behaviour which can be found in all his plays.

Neither Helena nor Bertram manages to come to marriage – or to continue it – with all four aims in harmony. And whether Bertram ever had procreation in mind (the only 'aim' he certainly achieved) is highly doubtful. As for Helena, any totting up of sums is forestalled by what the actors make of the spirit of the last moments of the play.

Although Shakespeare's treatment of gender and sexuality centres on the women of *All's Well*, and on Helena in particular, his treatment of these motifs in the male characters of the play is not simply an inversion. Perhaps the richest figure the play provides for speculation is its thoughtful fool. Lavatch, whose name suggests the playwright's placement of his views among the commonplaces of the barnyard, presents popular, if variously held, male views on women. Lavatch is sometimes labelled cynical, but his observations in Act 1 Scene 3 are less cynical than they are conventional. They repeat the traditional misogynist lore Elizabethans had inherited from the Middle Ages, the tangle of scripture, tale and pseudoscience that constituted the defence of patriarchy. Lavatch sings that although 'marriage comes by destiny' (according to the individual fate), the adulterous betrayal of men by women is inevitable since 'Your cuckoo sings by kind' (by nature). He pretends to amazement that the Countess's order that he fetch Helena is merely that – an order without dire consequences: 'That man should be at woman's command, and yet no hurt done!' And – much to the Countess's annoyance – he corrupts a ballad on the fall of Troy so as to condemn Helen rather than Paris, and he makes matters still worse by concluding that among women 'There's yet one good in ten.' The attitudes and their expression are traditional. Editors trace Lavatch's turns of phrase in this scene to proverbial tags, to mock-logic with long literary antecedents on the 'loving service' done in adultery, and to rather too obvious *double entendres* that were on every writer's pen. The scene has the air of a comic turn, part of whose amusement comes from one's acquaintance with all the jokes. Yet Lavatch has distinct, redeeming graces. Unlike the anti-feminist pamphleteers, he is ready to equate the insistence of his own sexual needs with those of his partner Isbel. As for marriage, 'My poor body, madam, requires it', and as for its possible disasters, 'If men could be contented to be what they are, there were no fear in marriage . . .'. If men are ready to accept betrayal they need not fear marriage. For this sentiment the Countess calls Lavatch 'a foul-mouthed and calumnious knave'. And so he is. But Lavatch's apparent resignation to adultery is part of his resignation to what is unmanageable in human sexuality in general, and thus to his equating of 'honesty' with moderation in his last speech of the scene (I.iii.89–93). His subsequent scenes with the Countess and Parolles make him even more of an almost-but-not-quite palatable, tolerant realist.

If the Clown's ballad is a warning against Helena, it seems arbitrary, but perhaps Helena herself is the ballad's one good woman in ten? One possibility is as likely as the other. More relevant is the general import of the Clown's comic turn. 'What power is it which mounts my love so high?' Helena had asked in her soliloquy at the end of Act 1 Scene 1. The answer she seems to have found two lines later is 'nature'. Lavatch's presentation of his needs certainly implies a view of nature, but one far different from the lyricism of Helena's soliloquy. Lavatch's comic turn postpones the Steward's revelations about Helena, but it is not merely digressive. It cues the audience to possible ways of rethinking Helena's past statements of her feelings and to ways of reacting to the coming interview with the Countess. It would be rash to conclude that Lavatch is the spokesman for Shakespeare's reductive irony, that Helena's love, by turns lyric, despairing and determined, is 'nothing but' the prompting of Helena's poor body, as such needs prompt Lavatch. One may perhaps be put off by the social overtones of the difference in rhetoric between Lavatch on Nature and the Countess and Helena on the same subject, the difference between bleak need and romantic longing. Is Nature only mechanical satisfaction below stairs and balconies and tropes for the masters? Or is this the difference in seeing that makes all things so? Parallels are not always parodies, and Lavatch's view can define an elevating distance as well as an undermining similarity. Moreover, Lavatch's attitude carries its own cancellation: it is stale, old-hat, easily dismissed as a bad joke.

Yet it is useful to examine Bertram and the depiction of male sexuality in general in the light of Lavatch's realism. The erotic range of *All's Well* is limited. There is none of the enchanted lyricism of Florizel's speech to Perdita in *The Winter's Tale* (IV.iv.135ff.), which culminates in the lines: 'Each your doing, So singular in each particular, Crowns what you are doing in the present deeds,/That all your acts are queens.' Petrarchan idealisations fuse movingly with a realistic acceptance of the beloved as she is. But where there is lyricism in *All's Well*, as in the speeches of Helena and the Countess, it is brief, too soon submerged in the practical necessities of the moment, and it centres in Helena on the physical, on arched brows, and hawking eye and curls.

Bertram's rhetoric in the seduction of Diana is predictably hollow, just what her mother told her to expect. He calls her 'titled goddess', contrasts his feelings for her ('love's own sweet constraint') with his feelings for Helena ('I was compelled to her') and speaks of his 'sick desires' even as the Countess has spoken so of Helena's. But Bertram only lusts after Diana – and that very briefly; he does not love her, and we may even question the 'purity' of his lust. Bertram was probably 'mad for her and talked of Satan and of Limbo and of furies and I know not what', as Parolles later tells the King. Yet he loved Diana 'as a gentleman loves a woman', that is 'He loved her, sir, and loved her not' (IV.iii.245). The King is enraged by what he takes to be Parolles' equivocation here, but Parolles is a more acute observer of society than is the King. He can see the workings of honour from the outside, more precisely the underside.

The trade-offs between love and honour in *All's Well*

have been noted often and variously interpreted. Their most pungent exposition is made early in the play by Parolles. Even before Bertram is married off he wants to leave his subjection at court and run off to the wars rather than 'stay here the forehorse to a smock' – a metaphor that hints that he views himself in a kind of femininising subjection as ward to the King. After the marriage Parolles seconds Bertram's resolve to join the wars by declaring that

> He wears his honour in a box unseen
> That hugs his kicky-wicky here at home,
> Spending his manly marrow in her arms
> Which should sustain the bound and high curvet
> Of Mars's fiery steed.
>
> (II.iii.275–8)

The relation between sexuality and honour is encapsulated in this elaborately graphic and wittily phallic obscenity that unfolds forward and backward from the phrase 'Spending his manly marrow'. If the erotic is a debilitating alternative to the gentleman's pursuit of honour in war, it should come as no surprise that the erotic can become acceptable if it is assimilated to the idea of conquest. Everything has been declared a surrogate for the sexual so it may seem strange to encounter sex used as a surrogate for something else. Yet if one wants to discover a 'likely story' for a Bertram apparently too immature for the responsibilities of sexuality who soon appears as the wild suitor of Diana, one can see it in seduction as the continuation of war by other means.

The Second Lord's speech refines the explanation: 'He hath perverted a young gentlewoman here in Florence, of a most chaste renown, and this night he fleshes his will in the spoil of her honour . . .' (IV.iii.13–15). The metaphor comes from hunting and Bertram's behaviour throughout the incident shows the seduction to be as much the conquest of an inferior (as in the hunt) as lust. 'I mean', he later tells the Second Lord, that 'the business

[with Diana] is not ended, as fearing to hear of it hereafter.'
There is no need to win a battle or kill game twice.
Conquering Diana once was enough. How much of
Bertram's 'lust' is specifically erotic we may well question.
The seduction of a social inferior such as Diana, the
daughter of a gentlewoman fallen on difficult times, was
the not untypical initiation into sexual activity of a young
nobleman. Victory in war was the conquest of equals;
sexuality, like the hunt, a conquest of inferiors – which,
finally, all women were. What ideal of marriage, if any,
Bertram held one can only guess at from the evidence the
play provides. Having, as he thought, rid himself of
Helena and established himself as a personage by winning
against both Siena and Diana, he seems content to fall in
with the socially acceptable and prudent connection to
Maudlin, a match into which we are allowed to doubt
that any romantic or erotic sentiments enter.

The relation of Parolles to Bertram in matters of sex is
even more ingeniously developed than their relation
in war. Again, one reflects on the other. Parolles'
condemnation of Bertram as 'a dangerous and lascivious
boy, who is a whale to virginity' is in the style of the
other revelations that are frightened out of him by his
mock-captors. But his reasons for writing his libellous
doggerel warning Diana against Bertram are as cloudy as
his reasons for attempting to recapture the drum. Both
place him in immediate danger of loss of life or livelihood.
Apparently he is unable to refrain from posing as a man
of honour or from opposing honour's code. Parolles
asserts that he intended the rhymed warning as an 'honest
[action] in behalf of the maid', Diana. Despite the letter's
cynical insistence that Diana make sure of her reward, it
is a gesture in the direction of fairness and underdog
solidarity very much like his advice to Helena to use a
good husband as he uses her.

T. S. Eliot found Parolles to be in the sinister,
threatening mode of Iago, a 'smooth villain', but Parolles
is more clown than menace, and his underdog sympathies

and his carping at his betters have about them a touch of decency, less of the maliciously self-serving than do Iago's slanders. Yet there is in Parolles something of Iago's envy, of his desire to serve his turn on his betters, that translates into a real delight in naughty revelations. This smacks of voyeurism, as in Parolles' testimony against Bertram in the last scene of the play. Parolles greatly enjoys acting as go-between in the seduction of Diana; surely going-between is in the very nature of *parole*. Only the fear of 'ill will' keeps him from recounting further details, but he would if he could, Parolles seductively implies (V.iii.251). Yet he has already told of 'their going to bed and of other motions, as promising her marriage'. What more is there to reveal? Only needless, deliciously indelicate details. The testimony of Parolles is a lucky but unnecessary addition to Helena's master plan for the entrapment of Bertram. But as does his earlier exposure, Parolles' unpleasant delight in the erotic serves as a contrast to Bertram's cool 'Certain it is I liked her/And boarded her i' th' wanton way of youth' (V.iii.209–10). As is appropriate to Parolles' name the contrast is between deed and word, but it is also a contrast between degrees of erotic feeling.

Bertram's accusations against Diana, that she 'did angle' for him, leading him on and putting him off with infinite cunning, are calculated to portray him as the sexual victim. This agrees with the only one we are allowed to hear of the warlike principles which the King imparts to the French volunteers in Act 2 Scene 1:

> Those girls of Italy, take heed of them;
> They say our French lack language to deny
> If they demand; beware of being captives
> Before you serve.
>
> (II.19–22).

Against Bertram's lies, which appeal to the commonplaces about the dangers of women to honourable men, and against Bertram's behaviour, which acts out the conversion of sexuality to an aspect of conquest, Parolles' concern for the besieged Diana, even mixed as it is with mischievous motives, shines hopefully, although it comes rather late and remains as words only.

Shakespeare's picture of aristocratic manhood in *All's Well* is more complete though not as profound as it is in the military society of *Othello*. At the centre is the idea of honour, with its prime attributes of physical courage and verbal honesty. Shakespeare represents honour's dark corners: aimless aggressiveness and brutal indifference to its consequences, hierarchical domination and its attendant exploitation of women and neglect of inferiors. Yet he also represents the comradeship of the camp and the nostalgia of comradeship remembered whose banter is an innocuous version of male rivalries. Further, Shakespeare gives us something of the fair-mindedness of characters like the brothers Dumain, whose regrets and condemnation of Bertram's abandonment of Helena and his attempted seduction of Diana are expressed in some of the most memorable lines in the play. 'Now, God delay our rebellion!', says the First Lord; 'As we are ourselves, what things we are!' (IV.iii.18–19).

This is a modest resignation to the fact of human sinfulness as expressed by the Doctor's 'God, God, forgive us all!' sighed out after he has seen Lady Macbeth walk in her guilty sleep. But for all the heartfelt concurrence of the Second Lord and his charitable insistence that Bertram 'in his proper stream o'erflows himself', Bertram seems no less a scoundrel of an *un*common sort. The last clause of the speech is thorny; the word 'proper' has paradoxical overtones of both excuse and greater condemnation. Somewhat later in the scene the relation between virtue and failing is looked at again, this time less drearily. 'The web of our life is of a mingled yarn, good and ill together', says the First Lord. Our faults, he continues, serve to keep us from pride in our virtues, which in turn keep us from despairing at our crimes. More soothing though this seems as doctrine, the play hardly allows us to apply it without strain to Bertram, though it is his treatment of Helena that occasions the speech. It seems a rather Pollyanna-ish way of saying of Bertram – as Helena has said of Parolles and as Parolles will say of himself in the final brief soliloquy after his exposure in Act 4 Scene 3 – that incorrigibility is fused with particular human endowments, and is not a barrier but even an aid to survival. If there is a fitness in Parolles' fixed evils, there is an unfitness in Bertram's *virtù*. With ideas of this sort, the perversion of love as an outcome of the need for conquest follows *not* from a social code that is presumably subject to change or neglect; it is made to seem in the nature of things, its intractability exemplified in extreme individuals such as Bertram. Presumably, however, the Countess is right and some of Bertram's behaviour is only 'natural rebellion done i' th' blade of youth', a rebellion for which others like the Dumains may pray postponement.

Male sexuality and gender in *All's Well* are largely sophisticated elaborations of Lavatch's observation on his body's needs and Parolles' paradox on how gentlemen love, loving and loving not. And instead of the glamour and hopefulness of the romantic comedies, the males of *All's Well* seem to face the grey prospect of acting on and being undone by natural impulse. For all this it is no oddity of taste that caused the words 'Monsieur Parolles' to be written in the 'catalogue' of Charles II's copy of the Second Folio, supplementing the title *All's Well*. The 're-capture' of the drum is one of the truly hilarious sequences in Shakespeare.

In retrospect it appears that Shakespeare the dramaturge has dealt even-handedly with the two sexes. Although Helena is clearly the single dominant role, she is almost entirely absent during the fourth act, the most entertaining of the play. The (nominally) male parts are varied and absorbing: the King, eloquent for the wrong reasons; Lafew, shrewd, generous, flirtatious; Lavatch and Parolles, each in his own way a truth-teller and a liar, each giving a complex account of himself; even minor parts like those of the Dumain brothers and the Countess's steward reward attention. Similarly, the nominally female roles are equally attractive to actors and audiences: the Countess, whose part Shaw thought the best ever written for an old woman; and the Florentine sisterhood of the Widow, her daughter Diana and their neighbours Mariana and Violenta – all welcoming and sympathetic to Helena, and each speaking part centred on a significant attitude: the Widow concerned for reputation and self-respect, Diana steadfast under insult, Mariana a home-grown moralist.

But as a poet Shakespeare has been less favourable to his own sex. The Countess's fair-mindedness and sympathy, the correctness with which she manages Rossillion, are far better examples of governance than the King's ultimately self-serving arbitrariness and elevated, if well-intentioned, ineffectuality. Her erotic nostalgia takes the form of sympathy for Helena; Lafew's the form of arch allusions to a potency neither he nor the King can pretend to. The nurturing quality of the scenes involving the Florentine women was admirably suggested in the BBC *All's Well* by their being represented as engaged in baking bread, a significant metaphor for their role in the play. The young noblemen are separate 'victims' in the husband-choosing scene, second Bertram's resolve to steal away from court by declaring that there's 'honour in the theft', and – most congenially – co-operate to good purpose in the ragging exposure of Parolles. But one must insist on the importance of the decent opinions of the Dumain brothers both in their condemnation of Bertram and in their fine reflections on his behaviour. Finally, one returns to Lafew, serviceable, unconfused as to where the right lies, yet charitable at last even to Parolles. On balance, however, clarity of insight, appropriateness of feeling and effectiveness of action lie overwhelmingly with Helena, the Countess, and Helena's Florentine allies.

Stage character is first and last a capacity to perform a role. In Boccaccio's Giletta all the capacities needed for the role of triumphant wife are assimilated to the force of love – natural desire, as the *Decameron* defines it. *All's Well* acknowledges natural desire as a motive of character and the engine of plot. But the social complexity of the narrative, dictated by the genre, the size of the work, the characteristic ways in which Shakespeare thought and wrote, encouraged no such singleness. His Helena is fully as honourable, passionate, discreet, daring, romantic, pragmatic, persistent and forgiving as her story and its particular shaping to its time and place require, but no more so. Bertram and marriage are her object, but for her to seek them in the contexts Shakespeare had created, losing her virginity to her own liking meant expressing an inwardness and behaving outwardly in ways unknown to Boccaccio's Giletta. In Helena role is not radically at odds with disposition as it is in Shakespeare's tragic figures. Yet role and disposition are not wholly at one; neither are the obstacles she must overcome gratifyingly weightless as they sometimes are in the romantic comedies. Indeed one obstacle, Bertram, seems unmoved even at the play's end. But in Helena Shakespeare created a young woman of great strength (his alteration of her class is evidence of his intention) wholly adequate to all the turns of his plot, a force herself rather than, like Giletta, the embodiment of a force. Through a careful use of soliloquy, comment by others, and her own language, he has tried to guard against the mistaking of that strength for selfishness or of her particular virtues for defects.

Comedy is the form of continuity and consolation, and women, biologically and historically, the agents of continuity and consolation. Appropriately women emerge in most comedies as the (theatrically) dominant sex. So it is with *All's Well* – almost. Their victory seems incomplete. No doubt if it were legitimate to imagine sixth acts we might imagine Helena successfully consoling Bertram. Yet the teenage hero of Siena would take a great deal of consoling for that one dark night in Florence. It is touch and go whether remembering its pleasures would lead to a victory of libido over chagrin – or unman him. But sixth acts are the prerogatives of playwrights and Shakespeare gives us only five.

Even those who profess satisfaction with the ending of *All's Well* feel called on to do a fair amount of explaining – or of highly loaded staging. Critics have pointed out that in the course of his career Shakespeare cobbled together many less than satisfactory endings; that even if *All's Well* does not end in triumphant joy it does conclude in hope (Robert Hapgood); that the conclusion is easier to understand if we view it symbolically (James Calderwood); that it allegorises the triumph of Venus over Mars (David Bergeron) or their mutual reconciliation and refinement (R. B. Parker); that Bertram is beginning to reform (Carl Dennis); that he is in fact redeemed by Helena (Eric La Guardia); that Bertram and Helena redeem one another (Michael Shapiro); that the play mocks such ideas (John Love); that *All's Well* gives us the limiting and precise application of a naturalistic vision to a magical motif (Nicholas Brooke); and that at the end Bertram is still a pretty selfish and stupid man, though 'cynical' is not quite the right word for the ending (John Barton). Gary Taylor in *Moment by Moment by Shakespeare* (1985) manages to have it both ways by arguing for the ending as an instance of Shakespeare's 'structural' cunning. Shakespeare succeeds whether or not we accept Bertram's change of heart; if we are convinced, well and good; if not, we only agree that fifth-act conversions (and the converts) are hollow. This seems an up-to-date version of Joseph Price's caution to both critics and directors to exploit the play's diversity, rather than forcing the play into a single mood.

Yet this is easier said than done. Bertram's progressive self-degradation in the last scene, the universal excuse and final condemnation it begets and the perfunctoriness and rhetoric of the last moments – Lafew's 'Mine eyes smell onions' and Bertram's doggerel willingness to love predicated on a clarification – demand a great deal of off-stage music, bended knees, extended hands and yearning looks to pass for even wan hope. But perhaps all this is only an exaggeration of the disparity between their knowledge of the bride and groom and of the significance of the ceremony that leads guests to cry at weddings. Yet if the ending of *All's Well* leaves open just the glimmer of a possibility of happiness, it is hardly commensurate with Helena's extravagant effort. Perhaps the implied caveat is a further reflection on the course of abject love in the Sonnets.

· 5 ·

Young and Old

For critics who find it a thoroughly impossible play structurally or even for those who think it seriously uplifting, *All's Well* can be surprisingly entertaining on the stage. Directors and stage designers give us the bustle of Rossillion and the formality and display of the Court, the fourth-act high jinks of what Hollywood calls 'service comedy', the vain, amateurish seduction and the bed-trick, and then the rhythmic crack of traps being sprung in the last act. Lavatch is droll, Lafew droller, Parolles incomparable. Yet in the reading, the play, like Parolles' French withered pears, can at times 'eat dryly'. It has also seemed too often to some readers to have a grey, valedictory tone. The adjective 'death-haunted' has been applied to the play and to its older generation, specifically the King, the Countess and Lafew – the last two solely Shakespeare's inventions. The whole play has been read recently (it seems to me) by the darkness visible of T. S. Eliot's *Waste Land*, complete with an impotent Fisher King and crypto-religious hope of renewal through the fertility of the new generation – the once-virgin Helena and the future-reformed Bertram.

Although in *All's Well* Shakespeare has obviously made an effort to distinguish between the generations and to contrast them, the kingdom of France is not represented as moribund, despite the illness and arbitrariness of its

King and his politic neutrality in the Italian wars. When cured, he rises able to lead a coranto, and later to act vigorously, first as prosecutor and then, though somewhat less vigorously, as master of ceremonies at the end of the play. Both the King and Lafew may have been 'worn out of act' but they are not worn out of thought or rhetoric or power to command.

Possibly some of this tendency of critics to find moribundity a settled theme in the play comes from the misapplication of detail, as in a concentration on the possible symbolic implications of the Countess's dark metaphors in the first speech of the play rather than on the losses, excitements and prospects of Bertram's wardship, which are the scene's reasons for being. Another prompting to the tendency is a neglect of the changed demographic context in which we come to the play. Death was at the centre of Elizabethan life as the cemetery was at the centre of the village; the analogy is Lawrence Stone's. Death was a frequent occurrence in persons of all ages, and was not something that happened mainly to the old. The modern association of death with the aged bears an odd relation to Elizabethan reality since relatively few died at a ripe old age (Stone, pp. 68–70). Only a minority of adolescents had two living parents, and forty per cent of the population consisted of dependent children. The bereavements of Bertram and Helena and their conjunction would hardly have been seen by Elizabethans as a dramatist's contrivance. If anything, we should say that Shakespeare's comedies are 'life-haunted'. The primary critical impulse to labelling *All's Well* as death-haunted and valedictory, however, is ideological. It is preparatory to asserting that the theme of the play is regeneration, that the chaste Helena's miraculous cure of the King foreshadows her 'resurrection' (hardly thought a resurrection by the audience) and the regeneration of Bertram.

Yet there is no doubt that *All's Well* has more than a comedy's usual share of death and dying, or that the elderly constitute a formidable, fully intended group in the cast of characters: the Countess, the King, Lafew, the Widow and – through their presence *in absentia* as needed models – the fathers of both Helena and Bertram. Unlike the elderly in conventional 'New Comedy' plots, in which the *senex* typically impedes the course of love and the older generation constitutes an obstacle to the efforts of the young to come into their own, the older generation in *All's Well* acts, for the most part, as aid and sponsor to young love. There is no meddling *senex*, unless one sees the matchmaking King of France, that particularly blind Cupid, as an enemy of love.

It would be a mistake to look for absolute contrasts between the generations, with the young conventionally feckless, madly in love or lust, riding off on adventures God-knows-why, full of skewed opinions and unsound attitudes, and their elders properly sage, well-intentioned, warm, balanced. Encouragement to see the generations in this extreme way may arise from the contrast between the play's least (Bertram) and its most (the Countess) sympathetic roles. Shakespeare's Iagos and Iachimos have about them an artificial glitter of staginess that insulates us from them. But there is no such remoteness about Bertram. His is the familiar insolence of privilege to be encountered anywhere, here accented for once by an inherited physical grace, nature conspiring with society as if to demonstrate inequality as an inescapable condition of life. Bertram too is a stock character, but from a genre perhaps closer to common experience than most such figures. Yet in both the young and the old there is a wide range of decent behaviour and psychological insight.

Shakespeare depicts the elders in *All's Well* lovingly and with respect, but he does not idealise them. In the person of an actress with the powers of Celia Johnson the Countess is a celebration of humanity. She is warm, sensitive in the anticipation of the needs of others, even-handed in managing her household. But she has another, less admirable if understandable, side – her conformism and passivity, and in the last scene her willingness to find excuses for Bertram. A touch perhaps too much of the 'proper' noblewoman and the mother both humanise and qualify what is a loving portrait. The care Shakespeare expended on the brushwork is evident in Act 1 Scene 3, before the entrance of Helena. The Countess's acute sense of domestic justice, the respect due social inferiors, the need to balance and preserve several dignities, are evident in her behaviour to her steward and Lavatch. She will have no revelations about Helena made in Lavatch's presence, but her epithets of dismissal – 'knave' and 'sirrah' – are followed by a comment on Lavatch's knaveries that is playful and self-deprecatory; it is an invitation to banter on that Lavatch accepts, dismissed or not. She is evidently indulgent of her randy clown and self-indulgent in playing his catechistical straight-man. When she dismisses him again, it is with the mitigating expression, again more invitation than threat, that she'll talk with Lavatch anon. In her amusement the Countess seems to have forgotten about Helena, as the Steward is forced to remind her. Lavatch continues his banter after a third dismissal, but because of the placement of the stage direction we cannot tell whether the Countess's 'Well now' (I.iii.93) is the mildest sort of rebuke to the still dilatory Lavatch or the most open invitation to the Steward. The Countess listens to him well, praises and thanks her Steward and, as earlier with Lavatch, tells him 'I will speak further with you anon.' In both cases, the expression suggests, without any violation of the proprieties of rank, a desire to soften dismissal with an assurance of need and respect. Of such a careful web of relations is the useful orderliness of Rossillion made.

Our earliest impressions of the Countess are sustained in the later acts. Her initial reaction in Act 3 Scene 2 to Bertram's letter announcing his intention to leave Helena is a denunciation tempered by concern. 'Think upon patience', she tells the French lords, declaring that adversity has strengthened her against tears. But when she hears Bertram's letter to Helena with its impossible conditions, she 'wash[es] his name out of [her] blood', first comforting Helena, then declaring her 'all my child'. Throughout the scene it is the Countess who with short, sharp interrogations discovers and probes the details of Bertram's action. Although she is willing to blame Parolles, she is careful not to excuse Bertram: 'My son corrupts a well-derived nature/With his inducement.' Her exit lines are a cryptic graciousness to the bearers of bad news: 'Not so, but as we change our courtesies./Will you draw near?'

Even more controlled and characteristic is her response to her steward in Act 2 Scene 4. The steward has accepted Helena's farewell letter informing the Countess of her pilgrimage in penance for her ambitious love, and – worse still – has delayed telling the Countess of it. The scene opens with a rebuke, 'and would you take the letter of her?', moderated by an initial 'Alas!' But several lines later the Countess is even more controlled and mild: 'Rynaldo, you did never lack advice so much/As letting her pass so.' The scene concludes with a longish speech instructing the Steward to write rebuking Bertram, and expressing the hope that, with Helena gone, Bertram may return – and Helena some time later. In this scene as in the rest of the play the Countess struggles to balance condemnation with love: 'Which of them both [Helena and Bertram]/is dearest to me I have no skill . . . to make distinction.' Her own feelings and confusions, however, never spill over into anger at her servants. So subtly was the Countess portrayed by Celia Johnson in the BBC *All's Well* that the nuances of character all registered, and one could not distinguish in her acting the distance of social status from the prudence of maturity or from the modesty and reserve of the essential person.

The other members of the older generation are sketched in less detail but all in some sense are like the Countess, sponsors and nurturers. The Widow is solicitous of her daughter's reputation and her own. She is persuaded to assist in Helena's plot only after its 'honesty' is demonstrated. Only then does self-interest win her over.

As the play continues, however, her exchanges with Helena grow warmer, as in Act 4, Scene 4, ll.14–16. But this is more a stroke in the characterisation of Helena – a sign of her power to attract sympathy – than in the characterisation of the Widow.

Yet the Widow is more than an instrument of the narrative. With a few small touches Shakespeare transforms exposition into character, naturalising the necessity of Helena's finding the proper allies for her deception of Bertram. In Act 3 Scene 5, the Widow spies Helena and identifies her as a pilgrim. 'I know she will lie at my house, thither they send one another.' But the Widow, who lives by renting out lodgings, having declared her indebtedness to word-of-mouth recommendation, is leaving nothing to chance. 'I'll question her', she adds. However, when Helena asks where pilgrims usually lodge, the Widow does not make a blunt, immediate pitch for trade. Over the sounds of Bertram's distant triumphal parade, she says:

> If you will tarry, holy pilgrim
> But till the troops come by
> I will conduct you where you shall be lodged
> The rather for I think I know your hostess
> As ample as myself.
>
> (III.v.39–43)

When Helena asks 'Is it yourself?' the Widow answers, 'If you shall please so, pilgrim.' These touches of wit and reserve temper the purposeful bustle, eagerness and obvious confidence in her hostel conveyed in the widow's first lines after she sees Helena. They not only suggest character tonalities for the actor's elaborating business but validate the Widow's later self-presentation as a gentlewoman fallen on difficult circumstances. For purposes of the narrative there was no reason to endow the Widow with any more than a house, a daughter and a willingness to accept money. Yet Shakespeare provided a frame for actor and director to build on, exercising their art in extending the hints of the text.

So it is with the older men in the play. Inevitably the behaviour and attitudes of the King of France are coloured by his role. Self-serving motives underlie, though they do not nullify, his passionate defence of virtue and talent in response to Bertram's initial rejection of Helena. His willingness to dismiss the supposed tragedy of Helena early in the last scene of the play seems as much embarrassed self-interest as concern for the feelings of Bertram and the Countess. But the reluctance with which he accepts Helena's medical services is based not only on his scepticism of her powers, but on his sense of responsibility. It would be offensive to his office and his own dignity to turn to quacks after his own College of Physicians, under royal charter, had been unable to cure him. Yet Helena's appeal to providence convinces him as it had earlier convinced the Countess. The King's last speech, the final speech of the play, with his provisional offer to Diana, 'If thou be'st yet a fresh uncropped flower', to pay her dowry when she chooses a husband, is a slyly comic *aria da capo*, a culmination of the play's account of the limitations of royal power when dealing with domestic matters. That the epilogue, which could reasonably be spoken by the King himself, opens by telling us that 'The King's a beggar, now the play is done' serves to underline the impression of ineffectuality. It also serves to recall sonnet 87, with its last line, 'In sleep a King, but waking so much matter', whose reverberations from dream to art to actuality echo again in Prospero's famous speech in *The Tempest*.

For all this, the King of France is a regular royal King. With the exception of the letter by Diana, which he reads in the last scene, and one or two short speeches during his conduct of the interrogation of Parolles and Diana, the King speaks verse. He can subject Bertram to sublime reproach, issue laconic commands as by habit: 'She does abuse our ears. To prison with her', play the canny magistrate: 'thou art too fine in thy evidence, therefore stand aside', and be gracious in forgiveness (as in V.iii.8–11). His diction and its cadence are consistently elevated and magisterial; he is a genuine presence. Yet perhaps his most congenial moment is his greeting of Lafew in Act 2 Scene 1.

The two old men are obviously friends of long standing, once comrades-in-arms. The civil forms are preserved; Lafew kneels before speaking. But in answer to Lafew's request for pardon, dictated only by protocol, the King replies with, 'I'll fee thee to stand up' – which ends all ceremony. From there on their exchange becomes one of ragging wit with the clear allusions to physical combat and the guarded ones to sexuality that are the cosy clichés of exclusively masculine repartee. The King submits to teasing, and himself teases in return, playing deftly on the words 'wonder' and 'imagination', and saying to us of Lafew's elaborate account of Dr She, 'Thus he his special nothing ever prologues.' All this is attractive on stage, especially if the King enters in a wheelchair or on a litter, as is often the case in modern productions. The light-hearted exchange not only provides a telling contrast to the intense and elevated seriousness of the interview with Helena that follows it, but portrays the King as himself serious without being solemn. This moment of human intimacy provides a context for the King's acceptance of Helena in the face of his better judgement, and a qualification of his later arbitrariness with Bertram.

As an acting role, however, the King is eclipsed by Lafew, a sharper, more varied character – one of the distinguished, battle-proven lords in the line that runs from the early plays to Gonzalo in *The Tempest*. Lafew is an upholder of the proprieties, but also a shrewd estimator of character, a ready cutting wit, and for all that charitable and open to sentiment. He spots Bertram at once for an ass, takes two dinners to smoke out Parolles, but is willing, if not to forgive them both, at least to see the world's work done. 'Mine eyes smell onions', his last and the play's next-to-last speech, is pure Lafew: hard-headedness and sentiment, propriety and radical under-standing contending with one another to entice the viewer into puzzling himself with possible equivocations and the actor into maintaining the sturdiness of the soldier while conveying the nuances of the ironist. Lafew is responding to Bertram's collapse into a dogged undertaking to love Helena should she make him 'know clearly' how she carried out the tasks he imposed, and to Helena's equally uninspired resolution to risk divorce should her explanation prove vague or false.

But just before Lafew speaks in the last scene of the play, Helena is given a line that, taken up properly – that is theatrically – is a genuine *coup de théâtre*: 'O my dear mother, do I see you living?' Has she suddenly noticed the Countess for the first time? What reason had she to think the Countess dead? The unexpected suddenness of it and the intensity it calls for if the line is to be at all meaningful place to the fore again the relation between Helena and the Countess – the most intense and moving in the play – with a consequent chilling effect on the reunion of Helena with Bertram. Perhaps more adventurous interpreters could find more than this – perhaps a fusion in Helena's mind of the 'natural' with the adoptive mother in the benevolent figure of the Countess. At this point, however, a word of caution. The line is too startling an appendage to Helena's last words to Bertram to be a mere fillip added to the general happiness. It can, of course, be thrown away. But taken advantage of, it can stunningly qualify the import of the reconciliation. This is no warrant to cobble together a deep-analytical revision of the play in which Helena is seen as really searching for her female parent. Yet it does force a backward look, a recognition that the affectional centre of the play is the interview between Helena and the Countess in Act 1. Only when she soliloquises about Bertram's dangers in battle is there a comparable intensity in Helena. But the primary effect of the line is local. And

here it works with the string of conditionals – the King's
and Bertram's – with Lafew's locutions and the enormity
of Bertram's lies to cast a shadow on the reunion of man
and wife. It is to these lines of Bertram and Helena that
Lafew reacts with:

> Mine eyes smell onions; I shall weep anon.
> Good Tom Drum, lend me a handkercher.
>
> (V.iii.314–15)

They are ludicrous in phrase, ludicrous in gesture. Lafew
continues by asking Parolles to wait on him. 'I'll make
sport with [together with? of?] thee. Let thy curtsies
alone, they are scurvy ones.' The precarious amalgam of
sentiment and implied censure in Lafew's first lines (in
verse) breaks into its separate elements of sentiment and
the no-nonsense refusal of thanks or submissiveness in
his prose comments to Parolles. Although Shakespeare
conceived of them as a generation sharing a moral
steadiness and a courtliness of manner, the Countess, the
King, Lafew and the Widow are figures whose multiple
contrasts serve to intensify their distinctiveness, aiding
and challenging the actors, and deepening the play's
illusion of verisimilitude.

Both Lafew and the King are principals in two passages
of *All's Well* that seem to pit the generations against one
another. The first of these is Lafew's reflection on the
King's recovery, the opening speech of Act 2 Scene 3.
The passage is cited in many contexts: as an instance of
changing Elizabethan belief, as illustrative of Shakespeare's
tendency in the Problem Plays to introduce ideas and
issues only tangentially related to the play *qua* play, as
an intellectual fulcrum on which the whole play turns.
This last view of the passage is generally held by those
who see the play as quasi-religious, emphasising the
'miracle' of the King's recovery, the (metaphorical)
resurrection of Helena, and the supposed regeneration of
Bertram.

They say miracles are past [Lafew declares]; and we
have our philosophical persons to make modern and
familiar, things supernatural and causeless. Hence it is
that we make trifles of terrors, ensconcing ourselves
into seeming knowledge, when we should submit
ourselves to an unknown fear.

(II.iii.1–6)

In this passage Lafew takes a position on a specific medical
controversy important just at the time the play was
written, and also (more obviously) a position on a general
philosophic question.

In a book now in preparation, David Hoeniger discusses
the medical contexts of *All's Well* in some detail; the
observations which follow are indebted to his work. Later
sixteenth-century physicians were increasingly 'scientific',
rejecting supernatural explanations for diseases, and in the
tradition of Hippocrates insisting on a search for physical
explanations. This position came under attack from
clergymen, especially those with Puritanising tendencies
and, more surprisingly, from the followers of the new
medicine of Paracelsus. The argument was complicated
by the accusation of some clerics that medical secrets and
cures for which divine inspiration had been claimed were
actually the work of the devil, an accusation in which
they were supported by traditional Christian Galenists. It
is useful to see this aspect of the medical controversy as
defining Helena's daring in offering the cure and as
necessitating the extremes of rational argument and
incantatory rhetoric that she employs in persuading the
King. Both the traditional Galenists (who constituted the
major part of the Royal College in Shakespeare's day) and
the 'new' Paracelsians had given up the King as incurable,
if we are to credit Parolles' remark. Their conviction was
so settled, in other words, that not even rivalry could
tempt them to a hopeful prognosis. Indeed, almost
universal opinion held that a long-standing fistula was
intractable.

This reference to the two schools of medical thought and the formulation of Lafew's reflections suggest Shakespeare's awareness of the controversy. His awareness of the larger issue – the question whether, as some Protestant reformers claimed, after Christ's death the age of miracles was past – was inevitable. It was the basis of Protestant rejection of the Roman Catholic worship of saints and of any 'superstitious' claims to miraculous powers. It resulted in James I's reluctance to employ the 'royal touch' as a cure for goitre, the so-called King's Evil. But again, as in the medical controversy, the 'purity' of both positions was compromised. Some extreme Puritan ministers and some Paracelsians insisted on the miraculous quality of certain events, among them the existence of survivors of the London plague of 1603–4. Oddly enough, then, on both the narrower medical and the wider philosophical issues, Lafew, essentially a conservative, might have found several rather uncomfortably 'advanced' thinkers on his side. It would be amusing to think of Parolles as possibly one of them; there are hints of his non-conforming thoughts elsewhere, as in his advice to Helena. In Parolles, however, conviction is controlled by opportunism (hence his agreement with the universal wonder), and both are controlled by the need for risk-taking to display his *métier*, the thing he is by which he thrives. Lafew is a dangerous bear to bait. Yet Parolles, though nominally in agreement with Lafew on the cure, risks playing young scamp to Lafew's old fogey. For this, after Bertram's surrender to the arranged marriage, Lafew twice rebukes Parolles in a most humiliating manner. The theme of both Parolles' mockery and his self-defence is simple: 'You are too old, sir; let it satisfy you, you are too old.' A lame reason for mockery and a lame response: Parolles has been bested by Lafew's shrewd judgement and force of character as he had been bested earlier by Helena's. He is far better at fantastic solo performance than at a debate over actualities. The occasion for introducing an ideological difference between young and old here is not taken up.

It is difficult to say whether Parolles' aping of Lafew's enthusiastic traditionalist interpretation of the King's cure is directed at the interpretation or at the interpreter. One is tempted to place Parolles with Edmund and Iago, as did Eliot, or even with Antonio and Sebastian, who bedevil old Gonzalo's Utopian speculations in Act 2 Scene 1 of *The Tempest* – all of them so-called New Men, stage counterparts of the young sceptics and opportunists for whom Lafew's unknown fears seemed gradually disappearing in the light of seventeenth-century science and 'policy'. Shakespeare's concern with the contrast, sometimes generational, as between Lafew and Parolles, sometimes not, as between Richard II and Bolingbroke, recurs throughout his plays and reflects a mind both attracted and repelled by the kind of figure suggestive of the pragmatic, sceptical ideas expressed at the turn of the century. But, as in the manner of the Problem Plays generally, the ideas are presented, the issues suggested – and then let go. They are not articulated fully as is the debate between Hector and Troilus on honour, but are left just as unresolved. By and large it is the play's most clearly sympathetic characters, the Countess and Lafew, for whom providence counts as an idea. The new world of policy and *praxis*, however, has no proper representative in *All's Well* – unless it is Helena, and she is of two minds about defending it. Helena is willing to trust to providence – *faute de mieux* perhaps – but she knows that God helps those who help themselves and so becomes a prime example of success in the new mode. Yet Shakespeare gives Helena inner moral scruples rather than the inner moral chaos he gives, say, Bolingbroke in *Richard II*, another character whose behaviour is unfailingly opportune, calculated and successful. In any case, Helena's goals are, to say the least, different from Bolingbroke's.

If we cannot see Parolles as the spokesman for a New secular against an Old metaphysical style of explanation, his aping of Lafew is more than a diverting comic turn. It does seem to display the providential cure as a theme for ridicule. Parolles' continual echoes ('You say well. So I would have said'; 'so say I too.'), insist on 'the brief and tedious of it'. His responses are more than the short to Lafew's long; they suggest a predictable, bromidic quality in Lafew's outlook, a view of the cure fit for a broadside ballad such as an Autolycus might carry. Here again Shakespeare seems, although equivocally, to undercut his story.

After Parolles' mockery comes the King's entrance with Helena, her choice of husbands, and then Bertram is hectored into marriage. This provides a heady and rapid contrast of moods, but the succession of events in Act 2 Scene 3, while exciting on stage, does nothing to make us accept Lafew's explanation. It remains mockable, if Lafew himself is not, and the cure remains a given of the narrative rather than evidence of some larger meaning.

To a great extent, however, our estimate of the miraculous nature of the cure and our response to Parolles' mockery will depend on the performance of the interview between the King and Helena in Act 2 Scene 1. Of line 129, the New Arden editor observes: 'The transition to couplets here marks the change to a more formal and less purely personal exchange, leading up to the invocation of the supernatural.' In performance the speech can be (and has been) 'milked' evocatively with cello-plucking or an electronic tone as Helena answers the King's 'Hopest thou my cure?' with 'The greatest grace lending grace', and then goes on to an elaborate circumlocutory figure of speech concerning Time of the sort that the Player King in *Hamlet* Act 3 Scene 2 speaks in the deliberately stale rhetoric of the play-within-a-play. But the lines can also be spoken as self-conscious and calculated artifice. At this point it is no longer possible for actor and director to postpone crucial decisions about the interpretation of Helena and of the play as a whole. And those decisions ramify backward to colour the speaking of Helena's first-act soliloquies and forward to reflect on how we respond to her 'pilgrimage' and the bed-trick. (However spiritualised the performance of the interview with the King, little spiritualising of the pilgrimage or the bed-trick seems possible.)

More commonplace than the intellectual controversies shadowed in Parolles' mockery of Lafew is the falling-off between the generations proposed by the King as he welcomes Bertram to Paris in Act 1 Scene 2. Bertram's arrival is an occasion for the King's self-pitying reflections on old age: the loss of friends and comrades and the sad difference between the likes of the dead Count of Rossillion and the young lords of today. For the King the difference lies in achievement and in manner. The young lords are full of jests, empty of action, apparently forgetful of the proprieties of courtiership and nobility, especially of *noblesse oblige*. In contrast, Bertram's father was witty enough, but expressed neither contempt nor bitterness, or – if he did – did so only on rare occasions when such responses were merited. And the responses were accompanied by action. His treatment of inferiors was respectful and self-denying; all in all, says the King, he was 'a copy to these younger times' which, if noted, would impress them with their inferiority. For once Bertram replies with some grace to the King's rather daunting introduction to his service at the Court. The King goes on to quote Bertram's father's wish not to live so long as to become the butt of the younger generation, who disdain all things not new, whose judgements extend only to tailoring, and whose loyalties are about as enduring as their fashions. This is the supposedly perennial lament of the old, and it elicits one of the perennial replies from the young: 'You're loved, sir.'

However, despite Bertram, despite Parolles, this lament over social entropy is a characterisation of the King, not of his kingdom. Only Parolles seems dedicated to fashion; his flying scarves brighten the stage, but become an emblem of pretentiousness. Insolent speech to inferiors comes again from Parolles and in the last scene from Bertram.

The wit characteristic of the young noblemen, at any rate one piece of wit that several of them devise and act out, is the collective plot to expose Parolles, something completely justified. More important is the genuine, almost choral decency, of their dismay at Bertram's treatment of Helena and Diana. Even from Parolles Bertram gets less than sympathy. Minor roles were, of course, doubled, and in more costumes than voices lords and soldiers condemned the fate of Helena and the crude attempt on Diana's chastity. There is a solidity in the Dumain brothers' emblematised, I think, by Shakespeare in making them brothers, that again forestalls any notion that the French nobility has in one generation gone from the heroic to the trivial.

Even in defence of Bertram there is a little to be said beyond his extenuating callowness and his entrapment by the King. Upon reading his mother's letter, obviously rebuking him for his treatment of Helena, he reacts as though he actually has a conscience. 'There is something in it that stings his nature,' says the Second Lord, who delivered the letter, 'for on the reading it he changed almost into another man' (IV.iii.3–4). Bertram's repeated enquiry later in the scene about whether the treacherous Parolles has said anything about *him* again reflects a tender conscience, or at least a concern for reputation. Bertram's changing into 'another man' is hardly a foreshadowing of a fifth-act conversion; here it is only a metaphor for extreme disquiet. For the most part, Bertram is as unattractive in this scene as elsewhere. He cannot share in the delight his comrades take in Parolles' virtuoso lies. When the First Soldier reads Parolles' letter warning Diana of him, Bertram responds with 'He shall be whipped through the army', and declares that before he hated only cats and now Parolles is a cat to him. He shows no appreciation of Parolles' virtuosity. Bertram manages somehow to be solemn without being serious.

Bertram, however, *is* the precocious hero of the Tuscan wars – for what little Shakespeare makes that worth –

and, having thereby laid claim to a recognition beyond what is due to his minority, is now willing to conform to the rules of the élitist game, especially since he thinks Helena out of the way. But to understand Bertram is not to forgive him. Shakespeare makes it clear that Bertram's contemporaries do not, though the loyalties of the camp and the hierarchy of rank lead them to say nothing to his face in rebuke. It is the older generation who find excuses for him. For the King Bertram was 'mad in folly, lacked sense', that is, he was out of control rather than merely evil. For the Countess his was a 'natural rebellion done in the blade of youth' when reason is overborne. For Lafew Bertram's loss of Helena is evidence that the greatest wrong he did was to himself. But then crude lies follow damaging revelations and Bertram is again condemned by all. With the appearance of Helena, however, the King's 'dismal thinkings' and Lafew's resolution to buy a son-in-law at a fair are dropped; apparently we are to have a happy ending. Presumably the earlier grounds for forgiveness apply once again – and with enough force to excuse Bertram's lies as well as his treatment of Helena. Given the circumstances and the swiftness of events, many readers and audiences distrust what they see.

There are no villains among the older generation, though with the exception of the Countess they are not quite paragons. The King's high-minded arbitrariness and self-pity are realistically observed. Lafew is a charming role, but there is an unpleasantly self-conscious archness about his sexual allusions that suggests the brave face put on declining potency. Nor are there really any deep villains among the young. Parolles is far too cowardly actually to be an Iago and he is driven less by personal ambition than by the demon of his peculiar talent. Of Bertram, as insufferable as he can be, there is a great deal of unlicked cub and sheer fool in him. The differences among the generations are not moral but simply generational. The young are climbing, venturing; the old have arrived. They can look down and with complete sympathy like

the Countess see their earlier selves in the climbers, or
see themselves only imperfectly and with regrets as does
the King, or even with hopefulness as does Lafew, who
calls Bertram 'my son, in whom my house's name/Must
be digested' when the marriage with Maudlin is still in
prospect. It is the old who are concerned with continuity
and strive to foster it, the women in the play more
effectively and consistently than the men. Their concern
provides some of the warmest and, in the King's fifth-act
offer to Diana, some of the most ironic moments of the
play.

The generational link was apparently intended as a
structural element in the play. The Countess and Lafew
are wholly Shakespeare's inventions and his King and
Diana go far beyond anything in Boccaccio. *All's Well*
without its older generation would be a far bleaker play.
The Tuscan war and the marriage of Helena and Bertram
might well have inspired Dryden's

> All all of a piece throughout,
> Thy chase had a beast in view,
> Thy wars brought nothing about,
> Thy lovers were all untrue.
> 'Tis time the old age were out
> And time to begin anew.

Yet the superior balance and maturity of the old, and
their concern for the young, though it is sometimes
wrong-headed or self-interested, suggest that from the
socially aimless activism of the young there may yet
emerge lives of value and significance. Each of the old
sponsors one of the young generation. While *All's Well*
offers few hints that the sponsors are simply patterns for
emulation there are grounds for seeing the play's extensive
structural alignment of young and old as designed for
more than a purely negative contrast. The Countess is a
special case, however. She sees herself in Helena, and one
does not have to endorse all the myths of the 'family
romance' to understand the particular satisfactions that

lead her to anticipate a marriage between Helena and her
son. It takes little imagination to see Helena, so controlled
in the face of Bertram's ill treatment of her, so modest
and sensitive in dealing with the Widow and Diana,
becoming in time a new Countess of Rossillion, as self-
possessed and even-handed as the mother-in-law she
replaces.

   In Act 1 Scene 1 the Countess tells her son, 'Be thou
blessed, Bertram', that is, I give you my blessing *and* may
you be blessed in this respect, that you 'succeed thy
father/In manners as in shape!' The next lines are cryptic:
'Thy blood and virtue/Contend for empire in thee, and
thy goodness/Share with thy birthright!' (57–60). May
your heritage contend with your virtues which shall be
the greatest – the implication being that since Bertram's
heritage is great he must strive for great virtue, with
'virtue' retaining the overtones of meaning of its etymology
in *vir* and of its cognate *virtù*. And may the goodness
you attain be seen as equal to your endowments in any
assessment of your character. This paraphrase does not
capture all the Countess's meaning, but it gathers enough
of it to point to her concerns. In both clauses of the last
sentence the Countess sees Bertram's character as an arena
of struggle, with blood and birthright pitted against virtue
and goodness as though for Bertram his station and
prospects, which were fixed, might well overbear a moral
excellence he has yet to develop. Of course the Countess
puts her views in as optimistic a way as possible, seeming
to equate the contending forces as if in emulation. But
she follows this particularised prayer with bits of traditional
Polonian advice and ends it with what seems like a slightly
defeated tone: "'Tis an unreasoned courtier; good my lord
[Lafew]/Advise him.' The passage is recalled in Act 1
Scene 2 by the King of France, who tells Bertram, 'Youth,
thou bearest thy father's face' and goes on to wish that
'Thy father's moral parts/Mayest thou inherit too!'
Significantly, the King thinks the resemblance between
son and father deeply intended: 'Frank nature, rather

curious [careful] than in haste,/Hath well composed thee.'
This may refer to Bertram's physical appearance in general,
but probably refers also to the family resemblance. 'Good
wombs have borne bad sons', we learn from Miranda in
the first act of *The Tempest*, but such villains as her
father's usurping brother are 'unnatural'. In Bertram,
however, Nature, if we are to believe the King, has worked
generously and with care. All this seems to promise some
hope, however tenuous. Bertram's responses to the King,
among them the assurance that Bertram's father's 'good
remembrance, sir,/Lies richer in your thoughts than on
his tomb;/So in approof lives not his epitaph/As in your
royal speech', are modest and well spoken. Indeed this is
perhaps the only occasion in the play to which Bertram
actually rises, not only in the gracious compliment he
pays the King, but in his rhetoric, which has the laconic
elegance thought characteristic of or at least proper
to formal, aristocratic speech. It is apparently hidden
somewhere in Bertram to be a Count of Rossillion in
more than name. While the possibility of his maturation
into the figure memorialised by the King is highly
problematic, Bertram seems to me less a candidate for
dismissal into happiness (Johnson) than for coercion into
decency. His lies, shameless in the sense of the common
epithet, are actually proofs – like his reaction to his
mother's letter – of a sense of shame and of the desire to
avoid it. This is at least a small beginning. That a Parolles
can turn into a Lafew is beyond possibility. But kept 'tame',
that is frankly enrolled as paid household entertainment,
Parolles' mischief will have found its proper sphere.

  If the older generation is seen as defining goals of
character and behaviour as well as offering support and
sympathy, the play's most innovative structural feature
suggests happy endings to come, happy endings perhaps
more easily accepted than the painful reunion of Bertram
and Helena and the salvaging of Parolles. This idea of
felicity postponed beyond the play was employed by
Shakespeare in *Love's Labour's Lost*, where, however,

happiness is certain after a fixed period of delay and a course of maturation. But if maturation, a theme typical of all romantic comedy, is suggested as an outcome in *All's Well*, it is suggested only tentatively. The ironies of the play's 'happy' ending are far more accessible.

Except for intellectualised satiric comedies like those of Aristophanes and Jonson, comedies end traditionally with marriages or their renewal, symbolic of the extension of the community. Had Shakespeare followed Boccaccio more closely and given us a fully staged public festival and the joyous revelation of a risen Helena with a babe in arms, and followed this by ungrudging forgiveness and kisses, *All's Well* might have been such a comedy. Music, dance, lighting and gesture and all the determination of actors and directors in league with audience susceptibilities can make *All's Well* seem such a comedy in the theatre. But the text has other directions. Only fifteen lines are used to introduce Helena and quell Bertram; his resolution to love and hers to give a satisfactory explanation are in the conditional and shaded by Helena's turning away so warmly to the Countess. There is none of the general pairing off as in traditional comedy. One may perhaps forget the luckily absent Maudlin, offered and withdrawn, but Diana's resolution at the end of Act 4 Scene 2 to live and die a maid, reinforced by Bertram's lies and insults under questioning, makes a double irony of the King's offer of a dowry. Yet it is Bertram's lies themselves that are most telling, in part because they are the path to Helena's triumph. He is still Bertram of the hawking eye, now even more dashing in a uniform. But the abject collapse of 'Both, both, O pardon!' with which he greets Helena seems to me as unattractive as the childish 'O my Parolles, they have married me!' with which he resolved to leave her. One may agree with the King that the bitter past, the sweet is especially welcome, and take the play's final couplet as Shakespeare's promise that all *will* be well. One may even hope that Bertram, remembering the satisfactions of the bed-trick, will reconcile himself easily to a fruitful and otherwise satisfactory Helena. Yet, as was suggested earlier, one might speculate with equal groundlessness that the memory of the deception would be emasculating. After all the seduction of Diana was part of Bertram's programme of self-creation as a man of power.

And what of Helena? She has achieved it all: preserver of the King, daughter-in-law of the Countess, wife of Bertram and mother of his child. She is no longer a poor physician's daughter kept on at Rossillion out of love and charity, but soon enough to be its mistress. The Steward will no longer spy, nor Parolles condescend. This is a great deal, but with it comes Bertram, and unless he is, or can grow to, more than the play has given us, he comes at too high a price for the Helena of daring, intelligence, passion and control who has fulfilled the impossible tasks. She has, in Benjamin Franklin's phrase, paid too much for her whistle. Yet perhaps this is the point: that she has paid the going price for obsession and social rank. That would seem to be in accord with the lesson of the Sonnets. Yet if Helena is reduced to ambition, she is mean; if to obsession she is pathetic.

Yet why reduce Helena or indeed any of the sometimes equivocal or ambiguous characters, events, passages in the play to some convenience of discussion or belief? The ending of *All's Well*, and the play as read backward from that ending, can perhaps be understood as we can understand the ending of *Antony and Cleopatra*, as an endlessly tantalising balance. When Cleopatra, about to join Antony in death, cries out, 'Husband, I come!', the play leaves us to puzzle whether this is the act of commitment and transcendence the play has so far withheld, or only the farewell appearance on any stage in her greatest role of the consummate actress whose infinite variety has delighted, bedevilled and finally killed her chief audience. So it is I think with the ending of *All's Well*, though obviously the human stakes and the author's achievement are considerably less.

If this *is* the case, it should not be an occasion for complaint that the playwright has bungled his task, giving us the comical-ironical-historical-tragical or comical-ironical-unthinkable instead of tragedy and comedy. 'The finale, strenuously composed though it is, seems somewhere to take a wrong turn', writes Jonas Barish in a brief but perceptive introduction to the Pelican *All's Well*. Barish localises the error in Shakespeare's apparent use 'at a critical moment . . . of an older, more schematic form of character portrayal' in 'a vastly evolved and elaborated context'. Yet Bertram at the end is too much 'the same Bertram as before'. Others have localised the difficulty in 'the evolved and elaborated context', convinced that Boccaccio's story sank under the weight of social and ideological complexity that Shakespeare loaded on it. Such views are taken to their most sophisticated conclusion in the position of G. K. Hunter in his New Arden introduction, a position that has until very recently dominated critical thinking about the play. *All's Well*, Hunter argues, is a late romance manqué.

Much of the perversity of the dénouement disappears if we see it as an attempt at the effects gradually mastered in the intervening comedies, and triumphantly achieved in *The Winter's Tale*, an attempt foiled in *All's Well* by stylistic and constructional methods inappropriate to the genre. The same theory explains much else that is perverse in the play . . . the odd combination of attitudes . . . its fairy-tale plot, its realistic and satiric elements, its brooding concern with problems . . . .

The case is brilliantly argued, but perhaps now seems less persuasive than at first. It seems to require a rather more prescient view of their development than authors generally have and deduces an intention from a failure to achieve it. Perhaps the strongest demurrer may come from questioning how narrowly Shakespeare considered stylistic and constructional methods 'appropriate' to particular

genres or even how far he was concerned to satisfy the
integrity of genre traditionally conceived. One might argue
from the evidence of the plays that he was concerned to
evade the constraints of genre and foil the expectations it
aroused, and that in some sense the late romances are a
falling-off from the complex realism and intellectually
exciting ironies of plays like *All's Well*. One does not
have to adopt Lytton Strachey's impish argument that the
later plays were Shakespeare's dotages to see the point.

Moreover, compared to Ben Jonson Shakespeare is
notoriously untidy in devising plots. For example, early
and late his plays exhibit a tendency for the character to
challenge the story, as Joan Rees has pointed out in
Shakespeare and the Story: Aspects of Creation (1978).
When this occurs through inadvertence and is allowed and
when it is fully intended is difficult to determine. Perhaps
saying that story is sacrificed to character or character to
story is not a useful formulation of the issues. In what
sense can we speak of sacrifice when the distinct impression
of both story and character remains, only enhanced by
the impression of their mutual violation? Is it not at least
equally helpful to see story and character as out of
harmony, jostling one another in a version of the familiar
disharmony between principle and pragmatic action,
between the ideal responses that situations seem to prompt
and what we actually bring to them? From the narrow
perspective of theatre this becomes the deliberate disharmony between idealised folk-tale or even genre in general
and an at-times almost parodically *un*ideal behaviour on
the part of the principals, in *All's Well* first Bertram, then,
more subtly, Helena. What Alastair Fowler acutely
observes in *A History of Literature* (1987) of the drama
of the period is true of *All's Well*: there is 'a special
disposition to toy with a play's framing or abutment on
reality, in such a manner as to confuse (or sharpen) the
audience's sense of where precisely the boundary lay'
(p.90).

Shakespeare is capable of treating all the genres as fairy-tale patterns on which reality at crucial moments focuses a detheatricalising brilliance. *Love's Labour's Lost* does not end like an old play; a year's 'community service' (so the courts now call it) must prepare Jack for his Jill. Feste's sad song is the epiphany that concludes the happy pairings of *Twelfth Night*, a play in which the universal rain that raineth every day seems for the moment to have wet only Malvolio. The pageant-politics of *Richard II* are reduced to farce in the Aumerle conspiracy scenes; the reign of King Fortinbras is the fruit of Hamlet's tragedy, and nothing in the reconciliations and restorations of *The Winter's Tale* restores Mamilius, or Antigonus or the (needlessly) lost years; Polixenes follows Leontes in irrational anger; and when Florizel is cautioned by old Camillo in Act 4 Scene 4 not to renounce his claim to the throne, he answers that he *is* advised – 'and by my fancy'. 'If my reason/Will thereto be obedient, I have reason; if not, my senses, better pleased with madness,/ Do bid it welcome.' It was *affectio* run amok that began the tragic events of the play. The suggestion is that the potentialities for tragedy remain. In Shakespeare the nominal patterns of narrative are not open only to the transformations of actual performance, but are sometimes shown to be unstable in themselves. Satisfying the demands of generic purity is generally an impediment to truth-telling. Nature, not as an abstraction but as actuality, had already broken in on the conventions of romantic comedy in *As You Like It* and *Twelfth Night*. *All's Well* is only a longer walk down the same path.

What is true of the mixture of genres holds also of the texture of *All's Well*. In *Proceedings of the British Academy* 67 (1981), E. A. J. Honigman finds Shakespeare's image of 'mingled yarn' suggestive of the principle of his art with its provision of different views of single characters; different emotions in a single phrase; past, present and future perspectives almost simultaneousely offered – all these making a given stage moment throb with implications. And, one should add, with the feel or at the very least with the illusion of the real that comes when representation is not reducible to simple statement. A good presentation of *All's Well* such as the BBC production under Moshinsky's direction can leave us strangely moved, as we are at many weddings, though we have no illusions about the couples and only guarded hopes for the future.

All's Well takes a mischievous and adversarial, if not quite a parodic, attitude toward its genre. Alexander Leggatt put the case succinctly when he gave his fine study of the play the subtitle 'The Testing of Romance'. Testing romance is precisely what *All's Well* does, and it finds romance wanting. The bare plot, as reassuring about the triumph of Merit as one could want it, founders when the Hero refuses to play the game and leaves Merit in the lurch. But the Heroine refuses too; Merit is not simply recognised, but for all its luck has to calculate and struggle and, unmeritoriously, cut corners to win. Just as dismal – the settings of romantic triumphs are the battlefields of a phoney war and a bed of assignation. Yet *All's Well* is still a romantic story.

All's Well is play self-conscious about language as well as about genre. This may appear to contradict received opinion, which finds one of the play's inadequacies in its failure to achieve a characteristic language. One should perhaps ask if this means that the language of the play is at some point inadequate to its task. Is the language of the King in exhortation unkingly?; the Countess ever less than herself, the human and thoughtful *grande dame*?; Bertram when his words are callow, cold, transparently false, or deflated not meant to be so?; the diction that conveys significant commentary on 'the tangled yarn of life' or 'the things we are' inappropriately gnomic and intellectually alert? The failure of *All's Well* to achieve a language recognisably that of *All's Well* is, I think, at bottom a demand for poetic drama, which *All's Well* is not. Making such demands underestimates the degree to which the language of the theatre is not the language of poetry, which in Coleridge's famous phrase 'calls attention to itself'. The language of drama is designed to call attention to something else – character, event, perspective – and poetic drama is accordingly something of a paradox, its language difficult to keep both poetic *and* theatrical. Despite its not being a poetic drama, *All's Well is* concerned with language.

As befits his name, Parolles is undone by words, by the 'chough's language' invented by the French lords to fool and terrorise him, and by the words of his own fantasising, either in self-praise or in deprecation of others. Both are language as play, language loosened from its immediate moorings in referentiality. Elizabethans were as much, if not more than we are, aware of language as an artifice and an imperfect conduit for thought. In several plays, *Love's Labour's Lost* and *Lear* among them, the treacherous inadequacies of language become dramatic themes. The closest that *All's Well* comes to thematising language is its insistence, through Parolles, on language as a delight in itself, an instrument not only as a tool but in the sense that a flute is an instrument. 'I begin to love him for this', says the First Lord after Parolles delivers a virtuoso passage of lies on the supposed lying and other indecencies of the First Lord himself.

The unimaginative Bertram, whose own lies to Diana leap from cliché to cliché with all the grace and inventiveness of hopscotch, cannot understand the First Lord's enthusiasm. Love Parolles for 'this description of thine honesty'? – 'A pox upon him!' Yet the rest of Parolles' audience wants more, and the First Soldier encourages Parolles to babble further. After another of Parolles' effusions on the First Lord's deficiency in military skills, the victim exclaims, 'He hath out-villained villainy so far that the rarity redeems him.' After a general unmasking, Parolles is left on stage to soliloquise that simply the thing he is will suffice to keep him since 'There's place and means for every man alive'. Apparently God must have not only his Saints but his Fools and Liars.

Later in Act 5 Scene 1, Parolles – exposed, humiliated

and rejected – appeals to Lafew and is saved. 'Though
you are a fool and a knave you shall eat', Lafew promises.
Yet his motive is not only charity. On Parolles' initial
plea, Lafew gives him a small French coin (cardecue =
quart d'écu) out of pity. When Parolles pleads to be
allowed to speak 'one single word', Lafew offers a 'single
penny more', but when Parolles sees the wit in Lafew's
equation of word and coin and finally identifies himself
by name, Lafew answers that now Parolles is begging
'more than "word"'. After further repartee Parolles is
adopted. From their earlier hostile encounter in Act 2
Scene 3 one might not have expected this outcome. Yet
it has been prepared for. 'I did think thee for two
ordinaries [meals] to be a pretty wise fellow; thou didst
make tolerable vent [verbal account] of thy travels', says
Lafew of Parolles. But Lafew's grudging admission of
having been amused is less important than his willingness
to continue a contest of verbal wit here and later when
Parolles pleads for help. When Parolles is called on to
give evidence against Bertram in the final scene, Lafew
intervenes to shield Parolles from the King's wrath at his
apparent equivocation.

Significantly, he characterises Parolles as 'a good drum,
my lord, but a bad orator'. I take this to mean not only
the obvious – a big noise-maker, but a poor persuader,
and one to be beaten rather than listened to – but also
that Lafew thinks Parolles a fine source and occasion for
entertainment but not otherwise a serious person. This is
his final word on Parolles, whose fate apparently is to
become to Lafew what Lavatch is to the Countess. In
denouncing Parolles to Bertram in Act 2 Scene 5, Lafew
has said 'the soul of this man is his clothes . . .. I have
kept of them tame and know their natures.' Parolles' fate
is in these lines. But the soul of Parolles is no more his
clothes than the soul of Lavatch is his. It is not only his
wit that wins Parolles some sympathy. Clowning is one
of the few careers open to wit, and to the intelligent –
Lafew, the First Soldier, the Countess and Helena – wit

is no mean gift. The final judgement on Parolles, the exposure of his infidelity and emptiness and society's toleration of him for the thing he is – witty entertainment – suggests the Shakespearian view of language recently proposed by Ekbert Faas: that words have no access to essential truths and can never equal what they stand for. They are the 'superfluous folly' that Helena sees taking precedence over a steely virtue. The instructive irony of such an aesthetic position is that it refers to a body of plays that by wide agreement are as close as theatre comes to the tenor of actuality. But the denigration of verbal truth, of the actor's skill (as in the Sonnets) and of the other mediating arts of the theatre (as in *Henry V*) is part of the pleading of the 'impossibility topos', the most easily accepted turn in the rhetoric of verisimilitude. Yet this too may be said for Parolles: under the surface scurrility there do seem to be possible hints of a genuine compassion for similar underdogs: the wife who has a right to reciprocity, good or bad; the besieged Diana; even the imaginary 'dumb innocent' that could not say nay to Captain Dumain.

Shakespeare rings several changes on the title of *All's Well*. After the bed-trick and her acknowledgement that Diana has yet 'suffer[ed]/Something in my behalf', Helena repeats this catch-phrase, remarking '. . . still the fine's [end's] the crown/Whate'er the course, the end is the renown.' The King ends the play, and repeats in the epilogue that 'All yet seems well' and that 'All is well ended' '*if*' the audience is contented. For Helena the catch-phrase is an expression of her reconciliation to the necessity of breaking eggs to make omelettes, as the rather ominous Russian saw has it. One will be remembered by the outcome, not the means. This is a pragmatic shrug at what one cannot, or what one chooses not to, judge more closely.

The King's phrasing is in the conditional in both instances: *if* the worst is over, then what is to come (the 'sweet' which seems also dependent on the King's *if*) is more welcome, a rather limp idea for the play's final couplet. In the Epilogue the catch-phrase is put to better use. The play is over, and the King has become a beggar once again, as have all the others, lords, soldiers, courtiers and women. But the actors' dwindling to reality and the outcome of the illusory fable they have presented have all ended well if the audience will applaud them.

Evidently Shakespeare gave considerable thought to what may seem at first hearing folksy throwaway titles such *As You Like It*, *Twelfth Night*, or *What You Will* and *All's Well that Ends Well*. On consideration *All's Well* has complex possibilities: the acceptance *faute de mieux* of what one prefers not to judge; a small hope for some future mitigation of a misalliance, an ironic reminder to those puzzled by his unromantic pair that it is audiences who decree happy endings no matter what. The title suggests a rather cool look not only at a fable of success but at the art of dramatic representation.

With the exception of the Sonnets, *All's Well* is perhaps as close – and it is, on the face of it, hardly close at all – as Shakespeare comes to writing 'A Song of Myself'. Shakespeare had achieved success in great measure by the time he had written *All's Well*. But the meaning of this success in the encounter with the social and economic obstacles confronting a young man of small beginnings would arguably have been as equivocal then as it is in any historical context once the obvious and substantial creature comforts have been allowed. Helena's only unequivocal accomplishment is the cure of the King. One wonders if at this point in his career Shakespeare had come to value only a healing art and so had a double sympathy with Parolles.

The principal characters of *All's Well* are not memorable, with the possible exception of the Countess. However much one reads (or writes), one returns to A. P. Rossiter's intractably two-particled Helena who allows no performance to be definitive, or to some other neutralising analysis. And an actor must be handsome and skilled indeed to forestall Bertram's retreating into a nasty plot device. The Countess, Lafew, Parolles, Lavatch, even the petulant Diana, provide more interest as 'characters'. Nor does *All's Well* provide many memorable speeches. Something of the same embarrassment about the undermining context that is evoked by recitations of Iago's lines on his good name or Polonius' advice to his son are evoked by the King's fine speeches on honour and merit. And Helena's ardent professions of love or concern for Bertram are songs that do not travel well from the text. The passages one recalls are snippets that warn against large generalisations and summary formulations; they see character and event as objects of wonder rather than understanding, life as a mingled yarn. For many critics all this, the cure of the King, the supposed death and reappearance of Helena, mark the play as religious allegory, an instance of holy chastity and spiritual regeneration. *All's Well* has 'a Christian (or at least a spiritual) colouring', to use G. K. Hunter's phrase. 'Colouring' is precisely the correct word. I think that the spirituality of the play goes no further. For all her faith in the efficacy of her father's 'good receipt', providence is the only widely acceptable justification for going outside the social and political rules of the game; for a nobody's independent and presumptuous appearance at court; for a King's overruling the jurisdiction of his chartered medical experts. It is, similarly, an acceptable explanation for the cure; even the College of Physicians could not baulk at it. Pilgrimage is also one of the few acceptable guises for Helena's travels, though they take her on the route to Florence, which few pilgrims would have followed. Of Helena's 'resurrection': before resurrection there must be death, and if Shakespeare keeps us in the dark about Hermione's 'death' in *The Winter's Tale*, he does not trouble to do so here. The audience's knowledge somewhat defuses the wonder of her reappearance in Paris. Spiritual colouration there certainly is in *All's Well*, but it is applied as a dramaturgic convenience in one of the more realistic and socially accurate of Shakespeare's plays.

All's Well, played as in the 1980 BBC production or in Trevor Nunn's Stratford-upon-Avon production of the next year, can be a memorable play despite the 'failure' of its characters to tap profound sympathies or of its language to yield passages that soar in the mind, and despite its hackneyed plot. It is memorable, I think, for its evocation of passages that arise in the course of all but the most dull of lives: being young and out of hope and then spurred to act by the least likely occasion; confessing the unthinkable and being accepted and helped by one older and wiser; giving up to illness in old age and then shortly recovering; seeing the freedom of adulthood beginning to open and then being snatched back into dependence. *All's Well* dramatises a folk-tale of the most extravagant kind, yet what other play of Shakespeare's refers so often to the vicissitudes of common life? Among Shakespeare's comedies *All's Well* is a singular triumph of quotidian understanding; it is the only fairy-tale we can believe in.

· 6 ·

Making it Theatre

In the reading of a play, its language comes to the attention large and distorted like a face in a convex mirror. The contexts of words become peripheral, the words themselves more completely abstractions that have lost much of the referentiality of speech. It is easy for a reader to entertain interpretations that are unactable or untheatrical: Bertram as a heroic victim, Helena as a relentless bitch, Lavatch as a foul dullard. Brief phrases repeated adventitiously across the breadth of five acts can be marched side by side as evidence of highly calculated thought, and isolated passages can be plucked from the page for interpretative argument. When the play is performed, however, all this is overturned. All the hidden contexts of language become visible; language becomes speech, its exact phrasing remembered little longer than it took to say. Eloquence is subdued as it merges with the substantiality and continued presence of thrones, doublets, the actor's face and form. Words spoken are shadowy compared to words on the page, which are sustained by print and repeated reading. But this solidity is gained at a price. Some of the unactable interpretations proposed in 'pure' reading *do* have an intellectual or aesthetic validity as examinations of the play-script as poem or as discourse. But if performance can lose something that is in the script, it can gain much more. Performance cannot simply ignore this or that 'inconvenient' passage, as reading can and criticism too often does in order to score points. Performance has to involve a whole text or reveal its bias by making detectable cuts. In its need to create wholes, performance unearths contingent meanings that even informed reading had not thought of. Yet despite its immediacy, performance, too, gives us less than the work of a major playwright allows.

There is an intermediate mode cultivated to some degree by everyone who reads plays: performance in the 'theatre of the mind'. Arturo Toscanini was supposed to have been able to sight-read a new symphonic score and hear all the instruments in his mind's ear. With some effort we learn to sight-read plays, hearing and seeing the nuances of gesture, expression and idea we attribute to the text. But pleasant and useful as this is, it is still subjective and self-indulgent, and finally just as unsatisfactory as 'pure reading'. Though we can legitimately analyse and discuss them as 'letters', play-scripts are intended as cues and clues to performance. The dramatist is committed to remaining the foremost, if not always the dominant, among equals, aided by actors and audiences and, increasingly at present, by directors and a host of technicians in the 'arts of the theatre', each of whom contributes to the significance of the performance. To say that the meanings of Shakespeare's plays are 'open' is a modern reinvention of the commonplace that even the 'legitimate' meanings and emotions which emerge in performance are not wholly determined by the text. But the theatre is not Liberty Hall. It has its own logic and logistics, and the play-script specifies some limits for performance and suggests others. *All's Well* can be played 'for' comedy or 'for' seriousness, even somewhat tragic seriousness, but unless the script is mutilated by cuts and additions, or simply overridden by perverse acting that, say, deliberately mocks in the delivery the King's speeches on virtue and status, the performance will be comedy of a particular sort, serious in a particular way, both intended by the author. It will not be comic as French farce is comic or Greek tragedy tragic, but mordantly comic, and serious with profound reservations as befits a play that seems to accept, even congratulate, little wickednesses and question and regret daring and success.

Typically playwrights attempt to control meaning in the theatre, especially to ensure against its being undermined by the actors. Hamlet's speech to the players is evidence that such attempts met then as now with mixed success. But the very fact of strong characterisation, of concreteness in statement and idea, is a kind of control, as is any precise articulation of materials. Moreover, the particular characteristics of good Elizabethan theatrical writing fix the playwright's meanings and tend to make them resistant to tampering. The first of these characteristics is the use of repetition without dullness – repetition with modulation – to compensate for auditorium noise and for the relative difficulty – less in that strenuously church-going age than in ours – of absorbing complex information through the ear. (Such repetition with variation extends beyond language to scene and motif.) The second is the invention of a language that implies gesture and movement, as in Helena's lines to the Countess: 'Then I confess,/Here on my knee, before high heaven and you . . .'. Its power to generate movement makes theatrical language seem the utterance of the whole person. It also controls the movement of the actors, much given apparently to 'sawing the air' – if we are to believe Hamlet's warnings. But Shakespeare takes chances, or rather he trusts his actors. He had to, and he was, after all, one of them.

The variations exhibited between the texts of his multi-text plays (those with one or more early quartos and a Folio-text) are sometimes difficult to class as printers' work, author's revisions or modifications made collaboratively in the course of production. In any case they suggest the obvious, that Shakespeare learned from theatrical performance. The chances he took with the

actors were also chances he took with audiences, who
varied also in their capacity to 'perform' mentally what
they heard and saw. The closer his scripts moved towards
paradox or complexity, the more his characterisations
centred on self-division, the greater the opportunity for
false emphases or simple wrong-headedness in the acting.
Shakespeare trusted the actors to take on these challenges.
In the so-called Problem Plays he seems especially willing
to take such risks. The problem of multiple or insecure
identity is a central issue in *Troilus and Cressida*. By
comparison, characterisation in *All's Well* is far less
complex, but the part of Helena, for example, allows
actors and directors ample opportunity to strike a variety
of balances between passion and calculation, submissiveness and initiative.

A third characteristic of Shakespeare's dramatic writing
is its dialogic skill. Shakespeare's earliest history plays
suffer from passages that are dull exposition, recited texts
rather than social discourse. Plays like *Romeo and Juliet*
and *Richard II* show evidence of a transition from poetic
writing, which 'calls attention to itself', to dramatic
writing, which is transparent, calling attention to character
and narrative moment. But beyond mere efficiency in
writing for the theatre is the particular quality that makes
for good dialogue. One of the highest if not the most
elegant compliments one modern actor can pay another
is to say that he or she is good to 'work off'. This refers
to the ability of an actor by gesture, phrasing, tone or
some other means to create a target space in his own
speech into which another actor's responding speech will
seem to fit exactly. In the modern detextualised theatre,
where successive speeches are framed to imply discontinuit-
ies or alienation, the creation of such speech-receptors is
to a great extent an actor's job. Shakespeare, however,
does much of this particular task; his dialogue is often
written with the interlocking shapes of a jigsaw. The
exchanges we have examined between Helena and the
Countess and the Countess and her Steward are cases in

point. Speeches follow one another logically, but they also pick up bits of phrasing from the speech before, using them as material for a revealing variation in tone and attitude. At the beginning of Act 3 Scene 2 the Clown tells the Countess: 'I know my business is but to the court.' Of course the 'but' is ironically spoken. The Countess plays off it in 'To the court!' as if amazed, and goes on, 'Why, what place make you special, when you put off that with such contempt', 'that' being emphasised. The added grace of dialogue here lies not only in the linkage, but in Shakespeare's forbearing to do the obvious and have the Countess simply echo Lavatch's 'but' before her 'To the court!' Typically the formula for linked speeches is verbal similarity, tonal and attitudinal differences. Compared to the resulting impression of the verbal and psychological grappling of social speech, Shakespeare's skills in writing eloquent oration and formal descriptive set-pieces seem, from the vantage of the needs of the theatre, only secondary ornaments.

In addition to its dialogic qualities, Shakespeare's language exhibits a peculiarly theatrical expressiveness beyond its conveyance of ideas and image. This theatrical expressiveness comes from a gift further developed by experience for sensing the proper length, weight, sound colour and balance of word make-up – say, opulence against restraint, familiarity against exoticism, formality against intimacy – in individual speeches and whole scenes. These theatrical aspects of language – its sound, rhythm and weight – often convey what audiences must know even before they can fully understand 'content'. The decorum and power of Shakespeare's rhetoric also plays a structural role. Often enough his plotting – certainly compared to that of Jonson – is careless or inadequate. Yet the consistent justness and vitality of his language impart an impression of unity and wholeness to his work.

Perhaps the most obvious of Shakespeare's skills as a playwright was his skill in choosing narrative materials that could appeal to his varied audience. There were, of

course, no guarantees, and *All's Well* evidently did not
please many. Shakespeare used a few comic motifs with
wide appeal again and again, varying their narrative
contexts and import. In *The Patriarchy of Shakespeare's
Comedies* Marilyn Williamson argues that the three
successive modes of his comic plays – romantic comedy,
Problem Play and romance – represent Shakespeare's
catering for the tastes and interests of his largely male
audiences. The social agenda of patriarchal ideology, she
argues, went through three phases, each of which elicited
a different comic genre. Yet his continuing transhistoric
popularity and the radically innovative nature of such
plays as *Hamlet* and *Lear*, for example, suggest that
Shakespeare created audiences as well as accommodating
them.

One has to think of Shakespeare's audiences in the
plural not only because of their differences in outlook and
sensibility over historical time, but because ideas of an
Elizabethan audience, an Elizabethan world picture, an
Elizabethan *Zeitgeist* or mind or outlook are library
inventions or classroom conveniences. Gabriel Harvey, a
contemporary, thought that Shakespeare's works 'have it
in them' to please both 'the young' and 'the wiser sort'.
In addition to age and so – by universal supposition –
temperamental differences, Elizabethan playgoers brought
further differences in conviction and sensibility to the
theatre. Yet Roman Catholic, Anglican, Puritan and
agnostic alike would have found something that reverber-
ated with their own views in that unresolved enigma, the
ghost in *Hamlet*, a goblin damned, a purgatorial victim,
a mere illusion. Those who drew monarchist or republican
lessons from the assassination of Julius Caesar – and
both lessons and more *were* drawn by Shakespeare's
contemporaries – would have found 'evidence' for their
views in the idealism (though tainted) of Brutus and in
the loyalties (though mercurial) of the mob, and in the
competence (despite its blind – or, rather, deaf – spots)
of Caesar. Looked at as an ideological statement, *All's*

Well gives some comfort to advanced *and* reactionary thought on the issues of class and gender. Helena *is* admirable and deserving, but also calculating and guiltily ambitious. Her ambition in any case is sponsored by the King. Her rapid ascent is based on literally saving the monarch and on her spectacular social conformity, even to accepting 'adultery'. Moreover, Bertram has become *déclassé* by violating the class code of personal honour; his word is worthless. The 'transgressions' of both Helena and Bertram and their results in a sense vindicate the status quo. The uneasiness of the ending allows actors and audiences alike to rebalance the tone and import of the play; now as the triumph of merit; now of brazenness; now as some ironic amalgam; now acceptable as the will of providence, now – enthusiastically or grudgingly – as the just result of superior intelligence and initiative.

Unlike Chapman and Jonson, who were arrested for offensive references to the Scots in a play called *Eastward Ho!* written shortly after *All's Well*, Shakespeare managed to stay out of prison. If so it was not because he was, as someone said of Tennyson's friend Arthur Henry Hallam, 'judicious to the point of nullity'. There is, however, an enormous rhetorical tact in Shakespeare's plays. A revival of his *Richard II*, with its depiction of regicide, was arranged by supporters of the Earl of Essex on the eve of his *opera buffa* rebellion against Elizabeth early in 1601. Despite this, several months later Elizabeth observed that she herself was thought to be Richard, adding rather petulantly that the play *had* been often performed recently. True enough, early printed versions of the play omit the deposition scene, but Elizabeth saw no need to suppress the play as was done with an adaptation in the 1670s during a crisis over the succession. Apparently she did not think it a partisan threat. It is no accident that Shakespeare was brought in to doctor the politically sensitive scene in *Sir Thomas More* dealing with More's handling of a rebellious mob. Shakespeare's rhetorical tact lay less in simple avoidance of partisanship – although he

168   *All's Well That Ends Well*

does avoid it – or in opportunistically bestowing bits of agreement on all sides than it did in a full articulation of character and event that revealed the intelligible bases of conflicting motives and the wonder of unanticipated outcomes. Inevitably, this pitted other elements of plays against the simple lines of their stories, making a charge of partisanship irrelevant. This follows not only because such plays articulate contending views, but because in this respect and in the integrity of their characters, whom Shakespeare shows as speaking 'in their own right' rather than as convenient expositors, such plays resemble the tenor of actuality in being irreducible to a single proposition or a point of view. They seem to be not opinion, but what opinions are about.

For all that, *All's Well*, as do the other plays, has its commitments. Its feminism should by this time be clear enough, as also its ironic questioning of abject love, martial glory and arbitrary governance. Elsewhere Shakespeare does not come down on that same side of these issues quite so emphatically; indeed he offers quite different views in *The Taming of the Shrew*. But *All's Well* is a good example of the fusion of tact and integrity that permits Shakespeare to manage materials that are 'relevant', and politically touchy because they are relevant, while avoiding both the bland and the partisan. One small model of his way of working is sonnet 129. All of the conflicting views on lust can be found in Textor's popular school-crib, the *Epitheta*; the paradoxical, radically analytic, conclusion is Shakespeare's own.

Among his less obviously professional skills are Shakespeare's tactful use of his company. Though a later date has been suggested, *All's Well* was probably performed at the Globe Theatre in 1603, a year when the theatres were dark after 19 March out of respect for the dying queen, reopened briefly, then closed again because of the bubonic plague until after April 1604, when they opened once more. Shakespeare's company (the Chamberlain's men, later the King's men – the name changed after they were given royal letters patent) probably consisted of 12 adult 'sharers' and four boys. Whatever the plots of his plays, Shakespeare – save perhaps in *Hamlet* – divided the telling so that there was only a reasonable burden on any one actor and so that minor parts were sufficiently interesting to challenge the actors and allow them to exhibit and develop their skills. What was sound logistically was sound aesthetically since the parts were thus contrasted for clarity and effect. Relatively minor figures such as Lafew, Diana and Lavatch are worth an actor's trouble. Even the forthright Mariana, who appears only once, has a fat speech that might enable a young actor to make his mark.

The two principles of dispersal and contrast that applied to the parcelling out of the story into 'parts' apply also to its disposition into scenes. The scene rather than the act is Shakespeare's conceptual unit; most of the act-divisions in conventional editions of Shakespeare's plays are the work of editors, and the evidence suggests that in many instances what are now thought of as act-divisions were simply swallowed up in the practice of continuous playing, frequently the case in the Elizabethan theatre. Those who argue for 'psychological' structures larger than the scene reach differing conclusions about format: two-part plays, three-part and four-part as well as the traditional five. Rather than pointing to an inflexible number of large units, the construction of Shakespeare's plays suggests a growth and then an unravelling of complication after a crisis, with each unit disposed into as many scenes as the particular play demands. There are 23 scenes in *All's Well*. The sequence exhibits a variety in setting, and in a number and type of persons, ideas, tone, verbal style, action and function.

Intimate scenes are followed by scenes in public places. The rowdy exposure of Parolles is plaited with the wooing of Diana. On stage the change in texture emphasises the parallel: two victims caught at the same time in matching traps. Some scenes further the narrative; others suggest ways of interpreting it. Certainly Helena's exchange with Parolles and her soliloquy in Act 1 further the narrative, as does her interview with the Countess. But the Countess's banter with Lavatch, with its rather coarse reflections on sexuality, serves as well as the chat with Parolles to suggest a darker view of Helena's obsession with Bertram. Some scenes or parts of scenes appear to be merely logistical, allowing for an impression of the passage of time, or permitting the playwright to avoid representing what would at best be awkward. One such passage occurs in Act 2 Scene 3 after line 184. The stage direction reads '*Parolles and Lafew stay behind, commenting of this wedding*', the wedding of Bertram and Helena. There is no reason why Lafew, perhaps even Parolles, would have been kept from attending the ceremony, but a great many reasons why Shakespeare chose to avoid staging it. An actual ritual, performed under duress, would have reflected very badly on both Helena and the King, and she in particular would have been unable to mitigate the damage by the kind of backing off that she attempted earlier during the choosing of the bridegroom. To be meaningful, her gesture now would have had to be no less than a refusal, impossible in any case. Yet had she made it, the marriage would have taken place none the less (this is after all *All's Well*, not another play), and both the King and Bertram made to seem even worse than before, the King's arbitrariness and the nasty pathos of Bertram's hangdog defiance further underlined by the ceremonial moment. Bertram re-enters after about 75 lines, barely long enough for a shot-gun wedding. Those lines are taken up by an amusing quarrel between Parolles and Lafew, a quarrel which continues even as it trivialises the age–youth theme and makes Lafew's later acceptance and charity to Parolles seem even more understanding and generous. In addition, Lafew's speech beginning at line 245 continues the concern with class and caste, particularly significant here because of the social transformation Helena is presumably undergoing off stage. For all this, the 75-

line stretch may seem too long to some, too much like filler necessitated by the decision *not* to risk staging the wedding. But in no case in *All's Well* is Shakespeare merely opportunistic; nowhere does he write passages whose only function is to place stage time between other materials. Few critics would argue now as some once did that Parolles is merely a get-penny humorist and Lavatch only rough stuff for the groundlings. Both, like Mariana, serve primarily to prompt us in ways of seeing events though they neither initiate events nor take an important part in them.

In individual scenes of any length there is also variety and much evidence of Shakespeare's *structural art*. A case in point is the long first scene (225 lines) of the play. At the outset it is public, formal and expository, announcing Bertram's wardship and contrasting him with Helena. The Countess's decorous concern for Bertram and Helena is contrasted with both Bertram's gauche behaviour and Lafew's smart rebukes. Then comes Helena's twenty-line soliloquy confessing her love for Bertram; private contrasts with public, intense personal feeling with formal exposition. Parolles then enters. His sexual banter with Helena, witty in idea and phrasing, goes on for 114 lines with an interruption by a Page calling for Parolles. After this the scene ends with a thirteen-line soliloquy by Helena, proclaiming her resolution to try to merit Bertram by curing the King. Parolles' long prose speech at his departure and his common-sense advice, 'Get thee a good husband, and use him as he uses thee', contrasts with the equally hard-headed but – in the penultimate couplet at least – none the less impassioned words of Helena: 'Who ever strove/To show her merit that did miss her love?'

This first scene is made up of blocks of contrasting textures. The number of characters on stage contracts from the initial four speaking roles to one, then doubles, then contracts to one again. The dominant emotional tonality alters as do the textures of prose and verse, each block deepening by contrast the impression made by the others, and so refreshing attention. The blocks are related in a variety of ways. Taken together they forward the narrative by defining the agents and predicating the main lines of action: Helena's force of character and her resolve to have Bertram, Bertram's attractiveness, his callowness and his lack of sense or manners, Parolles' ingenious unreliability, the Countess and Lafew as benign presences, the King as all-powerful. More than this, the successive blocks of the scene offer a series of unexpected overturns whose formula is the Aristotelian dictum that effective scenes be both surprising and likely. The second block of the scene – Helena's confessional soliloquy – is doubly surprising. The Countess's description of her paragon Helena, however, is overturned by Helena's private confession of her guilty passion. The contrast between Bertram and Helena in the first part of the scene makes her love for Bertram (of all people!) equally unexpected. (There is some point in not acting this naturalistically, in not having Helena make calf's eyes at him before her soliloquy.) Yet our understanding of the script and our expectations of theatre lead us to accept such surprises when they occur. Helena's interview with Parolles goes even further in undermining the early impression of her conduct-book perfection. Here is a Helena who can not only love a young ass for his curls but can trade off-colour witticisms with the likes of Parolles, and – here we come to the surprise of the fourth block – learn courage from the exchange. Helena's second soliloquy brings us back ironically to the strength and stature implied in the Countess's initial description of her. The successive revelations of the scene have fleshed out the Countess's report of this paragon, giving her the excellences of wit, a fullness of vitality and a resolution that is daring, yet not so daring as to go wholly beyond the proprieties. That she is *not* merely a Becky Sharp is some reason to expect her success.

The multiple functions of the first scene – as furthering the narrative, providing needed exposition, offering successive revelations of the central character and rewarding attention with varieties of textural contrast – furnish a model of how the composition of the whole of the play will be conducted. Contrasts of texture are apparent immediately in the scene that follows. We are no longer in the domestic world of Rossillion, with its primarily private concerns of individual maturation and individual emotion. The flourish of cornets, the elaborate costumes, the inevitable pomp around the throne and its knot of deferential attendants give us a court that dispels the domesticity of Rossillion with talk of war and diplomatic un-niceties. Yet the imminent presentation on stage of the Court and specifically the King of France had been placed in expectation by Helena's final couplet in the scene before, by her hitting on his cure as her means to Bertram. Such verbal links or if-then propositional or narrative links are typical of Shakespeare's scene-connections. In many productions the verbal and narrative linkage is visually reinforced as the King is brought in on a litter. Paris, however, is part of the world of high affairs of state in which 'little Helen' must succeed or fail. The apparently devious manœuvres of international diplomacy suggest an atmosphere that will necessitate all the tact Helena has shown in Rossillion and more. There is yet another difficulty: Rossillion was a woman's world; the Court of Paris is a man's.

Second in importance to organisation by scenes is Shakespeare's preference for large, polar character groups. The political plays pit rebels against loyalists; the romantic comedies court or town against country; particular plays, such as *Antony and Cleopatra* or *Troilus and Cressida*, Romans against Egyptians, Greeks against Trojans. In all these cases the groupings are thematic, but also suggest styles for costume, ambience, speech and movement. In *All's Well* the emphatic groupings are the most elemental ones – youth against age, male against female. The BBC *All's Well* caught the latter distinction perfectly in the macho gaiety of Parolles' exposure and in the nurturing care of the scene in which the Widow encounters Helena. At Moshinsky's direction, the Widow and the other Florentine women were first captured by the camera in the work and bustle of preparing the dough for baking bread. The grouping of casts around such thematic polarities is one of several structural devices Elizabethan dramatists employed not only to give the thematic weight of generalisation to their narratives, but also to orient the audience. Unlike classical tragedy, Shakespeare's plays are neither continuous nor linear in plot. Instead of a tight narrative sequence of scenes that follow one another almost exclusively in if-then propositional fashion, Shakespeare's scenes are loosely connected to their narrative line, relating the tale discontinuously and shifting from one group of characters to another, some of whom are linked to the narrative only as illustrative contrasts or as alternative interpretations of its events. Given this structural complexity and its accompanying tendency to de-emphasise sheer narrative as an organising principle, it was only natural that the major thematic oppositions in the play-script should have been clarified through character groupings which gave the audience its bearings. The encompassing of Helena by the bread-baking women of Florence on their first meeting affirmed the course of the rest of the play. The bread-baking 'business' was an exemplary piece of intelligent direction.

Perhaps the first decision about construction that the dramatist has to make roughly before he sets to work – and must continue to make in detail throughout the writing – is the determination of what to show, what to tell and what to imply. Some parts of the *All's Well* narrative *need* not be dramatised, some *cannot* be dramatised, some *should* not be dramatised. Often enough these categories overlap, and the playwright's decisions to show, to tell or merely to imply depend on many disparate factors that can include everything from fear of censorship to the particular talents and traditions of his company, to say nothing of the effects he wishes to achieve. Shakespeare

need not represent on stage the Count of Rossillion or
Gerard of Narbonne, Helena's father – and he does not.
He need not represent Helena's actual cure of the King,
nor should he do so. The sight of Helena burning dried
herbs under the royal nose, or mixing a potion, or rubbing
on a salve would vulgarise the cure and defeat its
supposedly providential aspect. The famous victories of
Bertram over the Sienese need not and should not be
represented; perhaps they *could* have been represented –
but such one-man devastations were a considerable physical
risk despite the excellent swordsmanship in the company.
Yet Bertram's exploits *should not* have been represented
lest they lose their shadowy quality with the result that
Bertram would become a more substantial hero, hence far
more a problematic and a potentially tragic figure (like
Coriolanus) than would have been useful for the humiliation scene at the end of the play.

It is even more obvious that the bed-trick itself *could
not* have been dramatised, *should not* have been (what
would be the point?), and indeed that the detailed
arrangements for it had to be handled largely through
omission. To have done otherwise would only have
emphasised the sordidness that, even as it is, reflects on
Helena, though Shakespeare's intelligent stroke in making
her regret the sordidness even as she revalues it into 'such
sweet use' helps to reduce the negative implications. In
any case, Helena's absence from Act 4 is obscured by two
absorbing events: the exposure of Parolles and the
supposed seduction of Diana, both of which have as their
secondary effect the placing of Helena in a good light.
Finally, Helena's long absence from the stage makes her
reappearance in Act 5 all the more telling.

Related to the decision to represent or narrate is the
ordering of scenes and within scenes the sequential release
of information. Shakespeare was not limited by the strict
chronological order of naïve narrative or the tight logical
order of Greek tragedy. His plays have a loose structural
syntax, permitting him to juxtapose scenes for textural

contrast or to alter chronological sequence to suggest
motive and meaning. Causes can appear after effects,
consequences before antecedents, making the narrative
more problematic, motives less certain than if the playwright followed a 'natural' order. One has only to imagine
the consequences of rearranging the blocks of information
that make up the first scene to see how differently
an audience would perceive Helena, or to shuffle the
supposedly extraneous passages involving Lavatch, or
imagine more stage time between Bertram's triumphal
entry and Helena's arrival in Florence or between the
attempted seduction of Diana and the exposure of Parolles,
to see the structural skill of the playwright in creating
dramatic irony and the suggestiveness of parallel meaning.
Having Bertram express a strong desire to run away from
the Court even before he is turned over to Helena by the
King obviously complicates our view of character and
motive.

A subtle instance of the programmed release of information occurs in Act 3 Scene 2, the scene in which the
Countess and Helena receive Bertram's letters announcing
his defection. The text makes it clear that Helena has
resolved upon action rather before the soliloquy at the
end of III.iii, in which she resolves to gain Bertram's
safety by leaving Rossillion. At line 55, as she hands the
Countess Bertram's letter setting out the conditions under
which he will accept her – the getting of his ring and the
begetting of his child – she says: 'Look on his letter,
madam; here's my passport.' Apparently it is the two
conditions blocking her acceptance by Bertram that
determine her travels. Only some twenty lines later does
Helena read the sentence that initiates her soliloquy: 'Till
I have no wife I have nothing in France.' The soliloquy
justifies her departure from Rossillion on the grounds that
her absence will allow Bertram to return to France and
so escape the dangers of war. Helena's expression of
concern is eloquent enough, but what we know of
Bertram's eagerness for adventure makes the reasoning of

the soliloquy seem doubtful, though perhaps consistent with some of Helena's imaginative views of her husband. The reaction to the challenge of Bertram's two conditions, however, requires no rationalisation. It is visceral and immediate. As she had set off for Paris to achieve the impossible, so she will now set off for Florence. It is too reductive to see either her concern for Bertram or for the King as simply rationalisation and afterthought. Helena is not so uninteresting a character, nor so uninteresting a task of characterisation. There is a Helena that appears not to see what the other Helena is up to, a selective self-ignorance that is familiarly human. Shakespeare carefully manages the sequence of information to achieve this complexity. First he provides the information – in only three words – that she's going to travel (the word 'passport' implies wandering specifically as a beggar); then as much of Bertram's letter as suggests why Helena must travel and what she must 'beg' for, and after a space the part of the letter that prompts the soliloquy and its self-sacrificial reasons for travel. A scene later we get Helena's letter to the Countess, which turns the journey into a pilgrimage and her sacrifice into penance and the 'embrace' of death. Only in III. v and vii, in Helena's conversations with the Widow, do we see clearly that she is stalking Bertram, and even then the relation between her plans and her pilgrimage is left for us to determine.

Looking back on the sequence it is easy enough to argue that Helena's self-accusation and professions of sacrifice are only window-dressing. Helena's letter to the Countess, with its rhyming end-stopped lines, its earnest awkwardness ('That barefoot plod I the cold ground upon') and its super-fervid sentiment, sometimes mischievously ambiguous as in the phrase 'sainted vow', does seem a bit much. And so it is meant to seem, since for purposes of contrast Shakespeare has recently given us Helena in soliloquy on these subjects and made the words ring true. In any case a hypocritical soliloquy would be a contradiction in terms. All this should return us to

Helena's first words in the play: 'I do affect a sorrow indeed, but I have it too.' As we have seen, the social anomalies of her position dictate anomalies of feeling and expression. What is specifically theatrical here, whatever its psychological or ideological validity, is Shakespeare's insistence on making it difficult to reduce Helena to a simple, moralising proposition. Like the people one meets, she does not come with a categorical description on her forehead. She presents herself as if in her own right rather than tempered and absorbed into a single narrator's point of view. The French novelist and playwright Montherlant said that when he was quite certain about matters he wrote novels, but when he held various or contradictory opinions he wrote plays. Recent criticism has made us see more of the problematic in fiction, but the drama continues to be the most open and problematic of forms, and so closest to the tenor of experience.

The structure of *All's Well* is unusual in at least one respect. The *All's Well* plot turns on the bed-trick; it is in effect the crisis of the play and should therefore furnish the 'obligatory' scene. Its absence reverberates as does the unstaged conversion-encounter of Hamlet with the pirates. Yet neither the bed-trick nor Hamlet's enlightening adventures at sea could possibly be represented. Perhaps the necessary absence of this fulcrum moment in *All's Well* is what makes the high jinks of Parolles' drum both necessary and satisfactory. In any case, the 'dramatic' or tense moments of the play are for the most part concentrated in its long last scene, Helena's exposure and final conquest of her husband. It is here that the sums and balances of all the accumulating details of character and incident will have to be made.

The final scene of the play is an instructive instance of Shakespeare's artful use of the interdependence of stage spectacle and language to establish meaning. The scene's uneasy balance of hope and doubt is vulnerable to new stage and film technologies that can readily tip the play into black comedy or exhilarations that may not have been intended, or possible, on the Elizabethan stage. In the introduction to his New Cambridge edition of *All's Well*, Russell Fraser writes: 'It may be a coincidence that when the [1980 BBC] television cameras in recent years have given us an *All's Well* that does indeed end well, the theatre has left us a touch more sceptical – "All yet seems well also."' The observation is just, yet perhaps the difference is not a coincidence but a result of differing techniques of production and directors' decisions.

Writing about the BBC production in *Shakespeare on Television*, ed. J. C. Bulman and H. R. Coursen (1988), G. K. Hunter states:

> The last scene in *All's Well* is a famous set of puzzles, as Bertram tries to lie his way back into favour and actually succeeds. The scene sharpens intolerably the play's basic problem of horribly real people caught up in a fairy tale – a tale for which a single ending will cure everything, the resurrection of Helena being transformed from a trick (which is what *we* know it is) to a miracle (which is what *they* think it is). The play comes to rest, that is, on the magical transformation of *their* world, and to this the director in some way has to subordinate *our* knowledge. What they see is that the light shone on them while Helena was alive is recoverable . . . the television production solved the problem . . . .

Moshinsky had the actors line up facing the door through which Diana is being led to prison. When she calls for her bail, music begins, and as she cries, 'Behold the meaning', the camera turns, not to Helena, but to the faces of the onlookers rapt in wonder. 'Face after face responds to the miracle.' G. K. Hunter was not alone in being moved. Even those who did not see Shakespeare's play-script as calling for anything like so decisively comforting a conclusion were deeply affected. That 'the play comes to rest . . . on [a] magical transformation' is arguable if only because Hunter is correct in thinking that the transformation, if it is to be achieved, must be achieved at the expense of our (the audience's) knowledge. '[T]ransformation of *their* world' is perhaps too broad a phrase; the issue in contest is specifically the transformation of Bertram, and the reappearance of Helena, however miraculous the camera can make it seem, is not a subordination but a diversion from that issue. It is, in any case, a diversion that is grandly effective in the BBC production, but unstageable. In the theatre the audience's knowledge that Helena did not die, but was very much alive and busily organising much of Acts 3 and 5, and its consciousness of the disgraced Bertram cannot be overridden by frame after frame of ecstatic faces. The stage cannot be so compelling psychologically at the expense of our consciousness of the whole social moment. And indeed had Shakespeare intended so strong an effect he would have employed means like those he uses in *The Winter's Tale*, allowing the audience, too, to believe Helena dead, and staging her reappearance with something closer to the metaphor and ritual Paulina and the Statue's presence impose on Leontes.

I suspect, however, that Shakespeare would not have been at all dismayed by Moshinsky's extremely tender last scene; he might well have quoted Robert Frost to the effect that 'The poem is entitled to everything in it'. The point is that although Shakespeare's text seems, to me at least, to demand a more problematic balance between salt and honey, the sonnet-writer's *sal* and *mel*, than Moshinsky gives it, his *All's Well* is a distinguished demonstration of the open nature of dramatic art, whose possibilities for realising 'new' meanings implicit in play-scripts only increase with new technologies. This is perhaps not a bad point with which to end, for when the playwright has done his best, it is finally his collaborators who must make the play theatre.

Select Bibliography

Adams, John F., 'All's Well That Ends Well: the paradox of procreation', Shakespeare Quarterly XII (1961), pp. 261–70.

Arthos, John, 'The comedy of generation', Essays in Criticism V. 2 (April 1955), pp. 97–117.

Bradbrook, M. C., 'Virtue is the true nobility: a study of the structure of All's Well', Review of English Studies 1.4 (October 1950), pp. 289–301.

Bullough, Geoffrey, Narrative and Dramatic Sources of Shakespeare, London 1958, vol. 2.

Byrne, Muriel St. Clare, 'The Shakespeare season at the Old Vic, 1958–59 and Stratford-upon-Avon, 1959', Shakespeare Quarterly X.4 (autumn 1959), pp. 556–67.

Calderwood, James L., 'The mingled yarn of All's Well', Journal of English and Germanic Philology LXII (1963), pp. 61–76.

Calderwood, James L., 'Styles of knowing in All's Well', Modern Language Quarterly XXV.3 (September 1964), pp. 272–94.

Carter, Albert Howard, 'In defense of Bertram', Shakespeare Quarterly VII.1 (winter 1956), pp. 21–31.

Cole, Howard, The "All's Well" Story from Boccaccio to Shakespeare, Urbana 1981.

Coleridge, Samuel Taylor, Shakespearean Criticism, ed. T. M. Raysor, London 1930.

Dusinberre, Juliet, Shakespeare and the Nature of Women, London 1975.

Ellis-Fermor, U., *Shakespeare the Dramatist*, London 1961, pp. 128–32.

Everett, Barbara, (ed.), *All's Well That Ends Well* (New Penguin Shakespeare), Harmondsworth 1970.

Fraser, Russell, (ed.), *All's Well That Ends Well* (New Cambridge Shakespeare), London 1985.

Guthrie, Tyrone, *A Life in the Theatre*, New York 1959.

Halio, Jay L., '*All's Well That Ends Well*', *Shakespeare Quarterly* XV.1 (winter 1964), pp. 33–43.

Halstead, William P., *Shakespeare as Spoken*, Ann Arbor 1979, vol. 4.

Hapgood, Robert, 'The life of shame: Parolles and *All's Well*', *Essays in Criticism* XV.3 (July 1965), pp. 269–78.

Hunter, G. K., (ed.), *All's Well That Ends Well* (New Arden Shakespeare), London 1959.

Hunter, Robert G., *Shakespeare and the Comedy of Forgiveness*, New York 1965, pp. 106–31.

Johnson, Samuel, in the Yale Edition of the *Works*, New Haven 1968, vol. 7.

King, Walter N., 'Shakespeare's "mingled yarn" ', *Modern Language Quarterly* XXI.1 (March 1960), pp. 33–44.

Kirsch, Arthur, *Shakespeare and the Experience of Love*, Cambridge 1981, ch. 5.

Knight, G. Wilson, *The Sovereign Flower*, London 1958, pp. 95–160.

La Guardia, Eric, 'Chastity, regeneration, and world order in *All's Well That Ends Well*', in *Myth and Symbol*, ed. Bernice Slote, Lincoln, Nebraska 1963, pp. 119–32.

Lawrence, W. W., *Shakespeare's Problem Comedies*, New York 1931, ch. 2.

Leech, Clifford, 'The theme of ambition in *All's Well That Ends Well*', *ELH, A Journal of English Literary History* 21.1 (March 1954), pp. 17–29.

Leggatt, Alexander, '*All's Well That Ends Well*: the testing of romance', *Modern Language Quarterly* XXXII (1971), pp. 21–41.

Love, John, 'Though many of the rich are damn'd: dark comedy and social class in *All's Well that Ends Well*', *Texas Studies in Language and Literature* XVIII (1977), pp. 517–27.

Muir, Kenneth, *Shakesepeare's Sources*, London 1957, pp. 97–101.

Nevo, Ruth, 'Motive and meaning in *All's Well That Ends Well*', in *Fanned and Winnowed Opinions: Shakespearean Essays Presented to Harold Jenkins*, London and New York 1987.

Ornstein, Robert, *Shakespeare's Comedies*, Newark, Delaware 1986.

Parker, R. B., 'War and sex in *All's Well That Ends Well*', *Shakespeare Survey* 37 (1984), pp. 99–113.

Price, Joseph G., *The Unfortunate Comedy: A Study of All's Well That Ends Well and Its Critics*, Toronto 1968.

Ranald, Margaret L. *Shakespeare and His Social Context*, New York 1987.

Rossiter, A. P., *Angel with Horns and Other Shakespeare Lectures*, ed. Graham Storey, London 1961, ch. 5.

Salingar, Leo, *Shakespeare and the Traditions of Comedy*, Cambridge 1974, p. 299.

Shaw, G. B., *Our Theatre in the Nineties*, London 1932.

Tillyard, E. M. W., *Shakespeare's Problem Plays*, Toronto 1949, pp. 89–117.

Turner, Robert Y., 'Dramatic conventions in *All's Well That Ends Well*', *Publications of the Modern Language Association* LXXV (1960), pp. 497–502.

Warren, Roger, 'Comedies and histories at two Stratfords, 1977', *Shakespeare Survey* 31 (1978), pp. 141–53.

Warren, Roger, 'Why does it end well? Helena, Bertram and the sonnets', *Shakespeare Survey* 22 (1969), pp. 79–92.

Wheeler, Richard P., *Shakespeare's Development and the Problem Comedies: Turn and Counter-Turn*, Berkeley 1981, ch. 11.

Williamson, Marilyn, *The Patriarchy of Shakespeare's Comedies*, Detroit 1986.

Wilson, Harold S., 'Dramatic emphasis in *All's Well That Ends Well*', *Huntington Library Quarterly* XIII.3 (May 1950), pp. 217–40.

Index